Temenos Touch

Evelyn M. Brodie

Temenos Touch: The Art and Science of Integrated Medicine and Non-local Healing

Published by Waterside Press

ISBN: 978-1-941768-57-0 ebook

ISBN: 978-1-941768-58-7 print edition

Illustrations and Cover Design by

George Christie

www.movingspiritfilm.com

This work is the explanation of my Temenos Touch Integrated Healing approach, based on the concept of the Temenos, ***'a protected physical and emotional space in which the transforming work of healing takes place through learning and teaching.'***[1]

[1] Buxton, Simon. 2004. *The Shamanic Way of the Bee: Ancient Wisdom and Healing Practices of the Bee Masters* p.28 Rochester, Vermont, USA: Destiny Books a division of Inner Traditions International

Dedicated to all the lineages of teachers I have worked with and learned from over the years

Peruvian Shamans	Don Francisco Don Sebastian Don Jose Luis Don Antonio Don Heberto Don Alfredo Donna Bernadina
Teachers in the Peruvian Lineage	Alberto Villoldo & staff of the Four Winds School Jamee Curtice Wake and Kinlen Wheeler Lila Hammond
Craniosacral Therapy	Thomas Atlee & staff of the College of Craniosacral Therapy, London
Rebirthing	Deike Begg
Psychosynthesis	Staff of the Psychosynthesis Education Trust, London Derek Mutti Cathy Warren
Reiki Masters	Paul Atkins 'Sean'
Tantra Teachers	Mahasatvaa Ma Ananda Sarita Martin and Hanna at Transcendence Yoga
Out of Body Journeying	Staff of The Monroe Institute, Virginia, USA
Deep Memory Process	Roger Woolger & staff of DMP training, UK
Meditation	Samyeling, Scotland Dhanakosa, Scotland Vipassana Centre, Chennai

Constellations Therapy	Albrecht Mahr Vivian Broughton Dimitrina Spencer Claire Crombie Sheila McCarthy-Dodd
Five Rhythms Dance and Movement Meditation	Christian de Sousa

And to my beloved George who nurtures me and encourages me to live the dream and continues to be my teacher every day.

And to Alastair and Katrina, who have been so supporting of their mum as she journeyed into a new way of being.

Contents

Acknowledgements

I give deep thanks to the friends and professional experts in various fields who read part or all of the early versions of this work and contributed such valuable comments and testimonials, especially Deike Begg, George Christie, Katrina Ferron, Dr Rosemary Gilbert, Carita Keranen, Andrew Klein, Joanne Perez and Cathy Warren.

I owe huge gratitude to Jasmin Naim for proof-reading the manuscript.

Thanks to all those at Waterside Press who have been of such assistance in turning my manuscript into reality.

And thank you to Dr Larry Dossey and Professor Ervin Laszlo who have never met me but who have been such inspirations and have been generous enough to provide their blessings for this work, whilst allowing me to lean so heavily on their years of research and experience.

I also gratefully acknowledge the following authors and publishers for giving me permission to reprint quotations from their publications and websites.

Buxton, Simon. 2004. *The Shamanic Way of the Bee: Ancient Wisdom and Healing Practices of the Bee Masters* Rochester, Vermont, USA: Destiny Books a division of Inner Traditions International

Dr Stuart R Hameroff.
http://www.quantumconsciousness.org/personal.html

Laszlo, Ervin. 2007. *Science and the Akashic Field: An Integral Theory of Everything (Second Edition)* Rochester, Vermont, USA: Inner Traditions www.InnerTraditions.com

Laszlo, Ervin. 2009. *The Akashic Experience: Science and the Cosmic Memory Field* Rochester, Vermont, USA: Inner Traditions www.InnerTraditions.com

Levine, Peter A. PhD. 2010. *In An Unspoken Voice: How the Body Releases Trauma and Restores Goodness* Berkeley, California, USA: North Atlantic Books

Lewis, Thomas, M.D., Aminin, Fari, M.D., Lannon, Richard, M.D.. 2000. *A General Theory of Love* New York, USA: Vintage Books, Random House. Reprinted in the UK and Commonwealth with permission of the Carol Mann Agency

McGilchrist, Iain. 2009. *The Master and his Emissary: The Divided Brain and the Making of the Western World* New Haven and London: Yale University Press

Mason Boring, Francesca. 2012. *Connecting to Our Ancestral Past: Healing through Family Constellations, Ceremony, and Ritual* Berkeley, California, USA: North Atlantic Books

Mason Boring, Francesca. 2011. *Walking in the Shaman's Shoes: A Transformational Walk with the Family Soul* www.revisionpublishing.org

Osho. 1973. *From Sex to Superconsciouness*: St Martin's Press/Griffin, New York, permission from Osho International Foundation, Switzerland, www.OSHO.com

Ruppert, Franz. 2012. *Symbiosis & Autonomy, Symbiotic Trauma and Love Beyond Entanglements* Steyning, UK: Green Balloon Publishing translated from *Symbiose und Autonomie*, 2010. Klett-Cotta, Stuttgart, Germany

Schneider, Jakob Robert. 2007. *Family Constellations: Basic Principles and Procedures* Heidelberg, Germany: Carl-Auer-Systeme

Sheldrake, Rupert. 2012. *Science Set Free: 10 Paths to New Discovery* New York, NY, USA: Random House Children's Books, a division of Random House LLC. published in the UK as Sheldrake, Rupert. 2013. *The Science Delusion* London, UK: Coronet, Hodder & Stoughton Ltd.

Villoldo, Alberto. 2005. *Mending the Past and Healing the Future with Soul Retrieval.* Carlsbad, CA: Hay House, Inc.,

Any errors and omissions are of course my own.

I would love to hear from any of you who read this book, especially if you have knowledge of areas where there is recent research that I am unaware of. Please contact me through balanceandpurposehealing@gmail.com

My healing website with full information about the individual services, trainings and workshops that I offer is www.balanceandpurpose.co.uk

Introduction

My first book, *Corporate Bitch to Shaman: A journey uncovering the links between 21st century science, consciousness and the ancient healing practices* was an autobiography of the events and experiences since 2004 that forced me to change my belief system and radically turn around my way of being and living.

Until then I was an economist, television journalist and strategic communications consultant with no spiritual belief system. I worked hard and played hard on the premise that when we die it's simply ashes to ashes, dust to dust, with nothing beyond life in this physical body.

Today I live and teach in London, England for about nine months a year, working as a integrated healthcare therapist. I treat people in an holistic way, helping them to release trauma, stress, depression, physical illness and the limiting beliefs of their social conditioning. I encourage them to step into their potential. I also teach a variety of workshops and training courses. For the remainder of the year I travel around the world to work with different teachers and take clients to Peru, to work with the Qero shamans[2] in the Sacred Valley of the Andes and the Shipibo shamans in the Amazon region outside Iquitos.

All the experiences I have had over the last ten years, with many differently induced altered states of consciousness and a variety of wonderful teachers, have led me (or to begin with at least, dragged me reluctantly) to understand that we are part of a universal, omnipresent energy, which in this book I will label the **inforealm**. This inforealm or energy field has

---

[2] My definition of a shamanic healer is a healer working with causes rather than symptoms, often in the energy field. It is someone capable of altering their state of consciousness to work outside linear space and time.

been called God, Brahman, Jehovah, Spirit, in fact there have been hundreds of different names for it over the millennia including the unnamable. In the present time this energy has been re-labelled in many new ways by specialists from different fields of science, medicine, biology and philosophy. For instance physicists call it the holographic or entangled universe, the cosmic information field or the quantum vacuum. Parapsychologists label it the psi field. Constellations psychotherapists name it the knowing field. In her pioneering work psychoneuroimmunologist Dr. Candace Pert calls it the inforealm[3] and in honour of her inspiration, that is the term that I use here.

In the early days when I started having experiences connecting with 'something' outside the physical body, my rational left brain was overwhelmed and fought desperately to understand what was undeniably happening to me. Since then I have been on an intense double track of investigation. On the one hand to experience a variety of altered states of consciousness and find out how best to use the information available in these states. On the other hand to try to find and understand the science of where this information comes from and how it reaches us: the physics and biology of an expanded consciousness. You could call it the needs of the right and the left hand sides of the brain respectively: experience and feeling versus information and understanding.[4]

My experiences personally and with clients have led me to understand that we are often kept small through our unconscious conditioning, limiting beliefs, family

---

[3] Pert, Candace B. PhD. 2006. *Everything You Need To Know To Feel Good* London, UK: Hay House

[4] Iain McGilchrist's highly acclaimed work, *The Master and his Emissary*, describes both the physiological and the functional differences of the left and right hemispheres of the brain in great detail. I explain these in Chapter 6, but simplistically the left brain excels at the tasks popularly associated with the masculine, such as logic, focus and compartmentalisation, whereas the right brain excels at the tasks of emotion, connection and seeing the bigger picture.

entanglements and accumulated and unexpressed (hence unresolved) trauma. My various trainings have also given me a huge toolbox of techniques that we can all potentially use to escape these conditionings and limiting beliefs. My scientific investigations have led me to start to understand how some of these apparently miraculous, drug free and frequently almost instantaneous cures of root causes, not just symptoms, actually work. Most fantastically they are not 'new age' wishful thinking. There is logical twenty-first century science underpinning them, although in the past, in the communities these techniques derived from, it was the practical result and not the theory that people cared about.

The genesis for this book came in 2012 when I went on a shamanic trip to visit Avebury, the megalithic site in Wiltshire that is home to hundreds of giant standing stones. At one point I was sitting in that place of Druid energies, with my back against one of the massive ancient stones, doing an Indian tantric meditation for the Earth with my Peruvian mesa (healing kit) open in front of me.

It was at that moment that everything came together for me. It became really clear that I can use all the tools from all my learning in an integrated and holistic way, to suit the life experiences, culture and difficulties of each individual with whom I work. That is why I have introduced an entirely new identity for my healing practice, *Temenos Touch*, as in any one session I may combine numerous techniques from many different traditions and lineages. Every client is unique. Every client has had a different life journey with different ancestors, conditioning, belief systems and experiences. Every client benefits most from a unique approach. There is no magic, one size fits all therapeutic solution.

The word temenos has different definitions in different dictionaries, including:
a piece of ground surrounding or adjacent to a temple;
a sacred enclosure or precinct;
areas within urban development that are parts of sanctuaries.

Carl Jung related the temenos to the magic circle, which acts as a safe place for mental work to take place. It is the place in which an encounter with the unconscious can be had and where this unconscious content can safely be brought into the light of consciousness.

My favourite definition, from Simon Buxton, opens this book: '*a temenos has come to mean a protected physical and emotional space in which the transforming work of healing takes place through learning and teaching.*'[5]

A safe space for entering the physical body-mind and also for connecting with the super-conscious inforealm or entangled, holographic universe is what I try to create in all my client sessions to give the potential for transformation and healing. It is also what I encourage others to create in the *Temenos Touch Training* programme that I offer to integrated healthcare practitioners (defined to include medical doctors, psychotherapists and alternative or complementary therapists).

My personal calling is to be a bridge between the worlds of psychosomatic and non-local healing (sometimes called complementary or alternative therapy) and the scientific, medical world. This book is an intimate weaving together of the accumulated learning and experiences I have had in the last ten years into one powerful, unified, scientifically based and proven healing practice drawing on many lineages and many branches of science and medicine.

On a practical and experiential level this healing practice incorporates information and exercises from shamanic traditions, particularly those of the Andes, the Qero and Alberto Villoldo, as well as craniosacral therapy, Reiki, tantric yoga, breathwork and meditation, constellations methodologies, trauma therapy, past life regression and modern transpersonal therapy. On a scientific level the training programme includes explanations of how these healing practices work, from renowned academic leaders and researchers within the varied disciplines of quantum physics,

---

[5] Buxton, Simon. 2004. *The Shamanic Way of the Bee: Ancient Wisdom and Healing Practices of the Bee Masters* p.28 Rochester, Vermont, USA: Destiny Books a division of Inner Traditions International

non-locality, psychoneuroimmunology, epigenetics and neuroscience.

This book aims to be both theoretical and practical, describing the why and how of a range of techniques which are most definitely not just for use by so-called new age or spiritual healers. These are techniques that can widely be used in an evolving, integrated, body-mind healthcare system that will hopefully become the healthcare system of generations to come.

My approach is cast in terms of Dr. Larry Dossey's[6] three Eras of Healing, which I discuss in detail in Chapter 2, but which in brief are:
Era I – mechanical medicine;
Era II – psychosomatic, body-mind healing;
Era III – non-local healing.

In Chapter 1 I quickly recap my story for those who have not read my previous book, *Corporate Bitch to Shaman* and I update my autobiography from where I left off, in the middle of 2011 until the spring of 2014.

Chapter 2 is a summary of Dr. Larry Dossey's three Era healing framework and the quantum physics underpinning non-locality and the inforealm, also called the holographic universe or the quantum vacuum.

Chapter 3 describes some of the modern neurobiological findings that are extending our understanding of the mind-body connection, with particular reference to stress and trauma. This introduces the 'why it works' behind therapeutic body work (Era II healing).

Chapter 4 describes some of the modern neurobiological findings that explain why our brains get stuck in old patterns and beliefs, through the formation of attractor pathways as well as the potential for change, derived endogenously through intention and exogenously through mirroring.

Chapter 5 explores the link between brain, mind and consciousness and new theories of the holonomic brain. This introduces the 'why it works' behind non-local healing (Era

---

[6] http://www.dosseydossey.com/larry/default.html

III healing).

Chapter 6 discusses the dominance of the left hemisphere of the brain in current society and the need to reconnect the body with the mind, bringing the left and right hemispheres into a better balance, so they may work in harmony rather than strife.

Chapter 7 considers why we all need to visit the shadows and acknowledge what we often hide away as being unmentionable. This applies above all to doctors and therapists who need to be as healed as possible themselves if they are to be of best service to their patients and clients and who also need to avoid taking on their clients' pain and suffering.

Chapter 8 looks at the space I aim to create when I work and the way I deal with my clients for optimal Era II and Era III healing. It also discusses what clients can expect in an Era II or Era III healing session.

Chapter 9 introduces Reiki, one well known and increasingly popular Era III healing practice.

Chapter 10 describes some ancient shamanic healing techniques, including illumination, soul retrieval, death rites and clearing psychic daggers, whilst drawing parallels between these and some of the techniques used in modern psychotherapy.

Chapter 11 presents a variety of techniques for working with past lives and the impact that such regressions can have.

Chapter 12 investigates the links between modern transpersonal psychotherapy, the massively expanding field of constellations therapies and the ancient shamanic healing traditions of working with the ancestors.

Chapter 13 looks at sexual wounding in a variety of forms, including abortion, abuse and addiction.

Chapter 14 explains why ritual is so important in Era II and Era III healing.

Chapter 15 moves into a selection of illustrative client case studies. In all cases the names have been changed and details have been altered and omitted to protect the identity of my clients. In some instances two or more people may have been conflated into one case study for illustration. I have also given all the case studies female names, as an additional layer of anonymity, although in real life they represent both men and women.

If you are a sceptic, I know you well and I welcome you! For my part I would never have believed ten years ago that this is the path my life would be taking today. But as I have learned from my own experiences and those of the hundreds of clients that I have now worked with, you never know what the inforealm has in store for you next.

Many of us like to believe we are in control of our lives, but we can never control what happens around us. All we can control is how we view and react to what happens. That **is** up to us and then our reaction has a ripple effect, as different reactions draw different responses from others. That is how we can create our own reality and why the same type of event can happen to a variety of different people with drastically different consequences.

I have no pretentions that this book or the techniques that I use and teach are **the truth**, if there even is such a thing. Everything here is based on my experience and knowledge at this moment in time. Both evolve constantly, as does all science and all experience. So if there is something you don't agree with, that is as it should be! Many of the teachers I have worked with will say that what they practised with clients a number of years ago is very different from what they do today. This work is developing and changing all the time, as is every particle in the universe. There are no right answers. There is only what appears to work right now based on our knowledge at this time; only what leads to changes that people appreciate and welcome in their lives at this moment.

But I want to live authentically, demonstrating the change that I would like to see in the world. As a result I feel compelled to offer this book at this time in honour of the many lineages of teachers I have been blessed to know and work with and in honour of the clients that come to see me every day.

My deepest hope is that I will inspire people, clients and

practitioners alike, to take a leap into autonomy, knowing that it is possible to make the future different from the past.

For clients this applies no matter how gloomy your situation appears to be right now and no matter what traumas you and your ancestors have suffered. Each one of us is in some way capable of magnificence, no matter what we have been told previously, but we are also capable of a tragic misalignment with our gifts. And claiming our potential usually requires us to do the shadow work first, taking out the painful wounds and looking at them in order to release their hold on us, stepping beyond the shame, fear, grief or whatever has blocked our progress.

For practitioners this means being willing to open your mind and explore beyond your usual areas of learned expertise. Now as never before, due to technological advances in medical imaging as well as the Internet, the amount of information available is expanding rapidly. Be willing to consider that the paradigm may be changing. In 2009 psychotherapist Allan Schore was invited to deliver a plenary address to the annual American Psychological Association Convention, which he titled, '*The Paradigm Shift: The Right Brain and the Relational Unconscious*'. He writes, '*At the present time a number of scientific and clinical disciplines are simultaneously experiencing a rapid expansion of relevant data and even a reorganization of their underlying theoretical concepts. Indeed the term paradigm shift is appearing in a number of literatures… An important contributor has been the rapid communication of information not only within but also between disciplines.*' [7]

The ultimate autonomy for each of us would of course be comprehensive self-healing, but often, particularly at the beginning of the journey or transformation towards a new way of being or a new paradigm, we need a helping hand or at least guidance. That is the **how** that this book offers to clients and practitioners. For those sceptical of any non-physical healing practices outside the old paradigm, it is also an

---

[7] Schore, Allan N. 2012. *The Science of the Art of Psychotherapy* p.52 New York, USA, W.W. Norton & Company

attempt to rationalise **why** an eclectic approach to healing 'dis-ease' is necessary.

If you are reading this you are probably living in a place and time that allows you to explore and evolve in a way that has often been persecuted and condemned in the past, and unfortunately continues to be illegal in certain countries today. If you have this freedom, I encourage you to say 'yes' to living in the fullest, healthiest, happiest, most knowledgeable, conscious way possible, using the vast range of techniques and information that are now at our disposal.

Part 1: Science

Chapter 1: Autobiographical Update

'If you work on yourself, you are already participating in the extraordinary, ageless work of overcoming darkness and pain, and of the evocation of latent potential. Take some time to realize that this work is not only your own private project, but the part of a wider unfoldment in which countless individuals are participating in many ways: the evolution of humankind.'[8] (Piero Ferrucci)

In *Corporate Bitch to Shaman: a journey uncovering the links between 21st century science, consciousness and the ancient healing practices* I told the story of the experiences that led me from the corporate world of economics, television journalism and strategic communications to being a shamanic practitioner, energy healer, holistic body worker, Reiki Master and craniosacral therapist. I explained why those experiences forced me, often reluctantly, to change my belief system and adopt a new way of living.

To recap briefly, after leaving Glasgow and Stanford Universities with a First Class Honours Degree in Economics, I spent the next thirty years competing largely against men in the driven, rational, intellectual worlds of government, the City of London, journalism and strategic communications advice. I worked for some of the richest and most powerful companies and people on this planet. For those years I stepped into the role of 'corporate bitch', largely suppressing my femininity, intuition and compassion, without even being aware of the harsh image I was projecting to the world and the damage I was doing to myself.

---

[8] Ferrucci, Piero. 1982. *What We May Be* pp227-228 New York, NY, USA: Jeremy P. Tarcher/Penguin

I now see that I was greedy, judgemental and selfish. I didn't really care about the problems of the world. My focus was on the acquisition of assets (greed), how I was viewed by others (judgement) and the comfort of myself and my family no matter what implications that had for others (selfishness).

I refused to acknowledge that I had held onto any of the religious beliefs of my strict Scottish Protestant lineage, but unconsciously I did hold onto the Protestant teachings and ethics of work, judgement and self-flagellation, which assisted me in achieving excellent academic credentials and a varied, interesting, and successful career for twenty years.

Throughout that time I firmly believed that when I died my body would be cremated and that would be the end of me. I thought I was happy in my belief that once my physical body was dead, there would be nothing else continuing beyond that, so I should enjoy life to the full while I could.

The journey I have found myself on during the last decade has come as a complete surprise to me! It wasn't something I had always intended to do. Until 2004 my dream was to take early retirement with enough money to buy a vineyard and a villa in Tuscany, then eat the finest Italian food and quaff the finest, (possibly home made) Chianti whilst watching the world turn around in the most oblivious manner possible.

But after stumbling upon a few pages in a book that piqued my attention in 2002, I got hooked into a path of enquiry that has opened doors that previously I didn't even know existed. And if you are reading this as a sceptic, please remember an exciting key fact: we don't know what we don't know!

The initial experience that changed my life came in November 2004, at a retreat centre in Wales, when, as a result of the aforementioned book, I attended a remote viewing[9]

---

[9] Remote viewing is the official term for the American 'Psychic Spying' programme that started at the Stanford Research Institute, (SRI) California, in 1973. It was conceived within and funded by the US Department of Defence and over time was known in the intelligence community as Grillflame, Centerlane, Starburst and

course. During this training, I **knew** my physical body was sitting in a room in the Brecon Beacons, but **something,** whether inside or outside of me, was experiencing events that were happening at a distant place and time. What was this something? Whatever it was, mind, consciousness, spirit or soul, my materialist belief system - that we consist solely of excited vibrating atoms comprising our physical body and that our minds are synonymous with our brains - had been shattered. What was this something?

Over the next ten years my quest to understand what I could not deny I had experienced led me to a huge range of experiential healing practices and altered states of consciousness (internally and externally induced). It also led me to the scientific areas of quantum physics, epigenetics, psychoneuroimmunology and neurobiology. I needed to satisfy my right brain and my left brain: feeling/experiencing and understanding.

Until 2010 I was still in full-time, corporate employment, so for five years I had an intense and exhausting period when I slept very little as I explored the all-consuming double track of experience and investigation. I seemed to need thirty hours in every day while my teenage children fended for themselves, subsequently inducing a considerable amount of guilt about having been a 'bad mother', which I have tried to atone for more recently. It was a conflicted time, with different aspects of myself pulling in very different directions.

Finally in June 2010, with my children reaching adulthood and independence, I quit the strategic communications consultancy I was working for and left for a seven month long trip, starting in the Amazonian region of Peru, working with the Ayahuasca plant medicine and the indigenous Shipibo shamans. I then moved on to the Andes to work with the Qero lineage of shamans and then after leaving Peru I travelled to India, Thailand and Laos where I worked with a number of different teachers from different

---

Stargate. It taught people to view military targets psychically, at a different time and place from where they were physically located.

healing lineages and traditions.

When I got back to the UK in January 2011, I felt ready to step fully into my new life as a shamanic practitioner, energy healer and body worker. I was driven by the knowledge that the teachings and lessons I had been gifted to receive were not just for my own use: they were for me to share with others.

I truly believe that the discoveries of modern quantum physics and neurobiology, particularly the implications of non-locality and the holonomic brain, need to be widely disseminated through our education and medical systems, if possible involving the media as enablers.

There is already a plethora of medical research about the benefits of meditation, human interaction, connectedness and various body/energy therapies, but this is not widely promoted to the general public or even the medical profession.

Undoubtedly the lack of public awareness of modern science and medicine is partly because some of the physics and language is difficult to understand and conflicts with our day-to-day understanding of reality.

But it is also because the ancient paradigm of power and control is still at large in our world. The vested interests of the pharmaceutical industry, the various religious institutions and the medical establishment would stand to lose money, power and influence if citizens were given accurate and complete information about the extent to which they can take responsibility for their own health and wellbeing and the extent to which they are kept small and controlled by these establishments. Our entire educational philosophy and infrastructure would be heavily impacted if this knowledge became widespread, involving a huge disruption and re-training to a new mind-set.

So there are huge vested interests in perpetuating ignorance and the status quo. But gradually all old paradigms are shaken and over-turned, and the anomalies appearing within the current paradigm are mounting towards a critical level, after which they will not be capable of being pushed under the carpet and ignored any longer.

At the individual level, for many people it is much more convenient and comfortable to point a finger and blame others for their misfortunes, rather than taking personal responsibility for their situation. Being a victim can have its advantages! Bert Hellinger is the psychotherapist who developed the constellations method of therapy in the 1980s, in which the facilitator (the therapist) sees the client in the context of their family and tribe, not just as isolated individuals. He describes very clearly two reasons why we often choose to be victims and hold onto our pain.

First, *'Suffering with a problem is easier to bear than a resolution. That has to do with the fact that suffering and continuing to carry a problem are deeply bound to a feeling of innocence and loyalty at a magical level. It is the deep hope that through one's own suffering another person will be rescued.'*[10]

Secondly, *'There is also a widespread notion that if I suffer long enough for something, it must be right. That is justifying the suffering rather than admitting that it's high time I moved on to something else.'*[11]

A third reason is that it may feel easier, or even more enjoyable in the short term, to abdicate self-responsibility and adopt a victim position. To take the attitude that *'It's not my fault. My parents are to blame. My boyfriend/girlfriend is to blame. It's my boss' fault. It's McDonalds' fault. It's my genetics.'* In the short term I might feel as if I get more pleasure from just sitting in front of the TV with a bottle of wine and a large pizza or a tub of ice cream than I get from going out to the gym to do a yoga class followed by a meditation, or running around the local park in the pouring rain then coming home to cook quinoa with fresh vegetables.

But we do all have choice. Choice plays a much bigger part for most of us than we often care to admit, including the choice to be depressed, fat, addicted or unhealthy. One of the

---

[10] Hellinger, Bert with ten Hovel, Gabriele. 1999. *Acknowledging What Is* p.11 Phoenix, Arizona, USA: Zeig, Tucker & Co., Inc.
[11] Hellinger, Bert with ten Hovel, Gabriele. 1999. *Acknowledging What Is* p.27 Phoenix, Arizona, USA: Zeig, Tucker & Co., Inc.

steps towards having a more satisfying, authentic life is to take responsibility for the choices we make. When we stop blaming circumstances, genes, parents or even McDonalds for our depression, body weight/shape, addictions or sickness, we remove a set of self-imposed limits. We are not victims unless we choose to be.

In Simon Buxton's book he quotes words spoken to him by his teacher, the Bee Master, '*The human being carries one primary human right and one primary human duty. One cannot be separated from the other; indeed, they are two sides of the human coin. The right that should be bestowed upon all human beings is the right to do as you please. However, hand in hand with this right comes the basic human duty, which is that you must accept the consequences.*'[12]

I am aware that this may sound harsh and I would like to make it clear that I'm not saying that everyone who is ill or disabled has brought that upon themselves. Of course there are accidents and there may be disabilities right from the moment of conception. But even then there is choice about how to react to the circumstances we find ourselves in. If we accept that we always have the right to do as we please, in the circumstances we find ourselves in, accompanied by the duty to accept the consequences of our actions, then we are no longer victims of anything and we attain a sense of power and freedom.

However, if we choose to be healthy in mind, body and spirit, it does take a certain amount of will and effort. People don't run a marathon, win an event at the Olympics, become chief executive of a company, or compose a symphony, without significant training and focus. We can all make a huge difference to our personal health and wellbeing **if** we take self-responsibility. Everything has consequences and we shouldn't moan about those consequences when we made the choice about how to react to the events around us and how to

---

[12] Buxton, Simon. 2004. *The Shamanic Way of the Bee: Ancient Wisdom and Healing Practices of the Bee Masters* pp163-164 Rochester, Vermont, USA: Destiny Books a division of Inner Traditions International

spend our evenings and our weekends.

Continuing my own personal work and story

Corporate Bitch to Shaman finished shortly after my return to London in January 2011. I worked in London again until September 2011 and then left the UK for another four-month trip overseas. After visiting my daughter in California, I headed to Nepal to hike the Annapurna trail, a twenty-two day circular trek starting and finishing in Pokhara. That was a really tough experience, hiking to an altitude of 5,416 metres. I was forced to dig into my physical resources in a way I had never done before, but it was also stunningly beautiful and increased my appreciation for this amazing planet we live on.

From Nepal I took the train to India, to work again with Ma Ananda Sarita[13] at Osho Nisarga, in the second installment of her three-part course to bring to life through one hundred and twelve meditations, Osho's tantric masterpiece, *The Book of Secrets*.[14] This gave me further personal growth and awareness as well as demonstrating additional techniques that I use in my work with clients, which unfortunately frequently involves issues of sexual abuse or wounding.

I came back to the UK from that journey in January 2012, and embarked on a year-long training course in constellations therapies based in Oxford, which has given me further great insights and tools, many of which I discuss in this book.

On a personal level, my ex-lover and best friend George picked me up at the airport when I arrived back from India and 2012 became another year of huge emotional learning for me.

George and I started spending more and more time together again, but he was still very clear that he wanted

---

[13] http://www.ananda-sarita.com

[14] Osho. 1974. *The Book of Secrets: 112 Meditations to Discover the Mystery Within* New York, NY, USA: Osho International Foundation

children and as a result we were just friends for nine months. That was incredibly difficult for me, as I still loved him dearly, and desired a resumption of our previous sexual relationship, but he was totally honourable and said that if he started sleeping with me again, it would distract him from his intention to find a woman to be the mother of his children. He never wanted to be unfaithful to me or betray me. However, as we spent more and more time together again, the love between us deepened even further.

By September I was planning my next trip back to Peru to learn Spanish and work again with the shamans in the Andes. All of a sudden through a change in his circumstances George decided that he wanted to come with me again to Peru, as he did in 2010, and we resumed our love affair, followed by an amazing time of bonding and working with the plant medicine in Cusco and Lake Titicaca.

In January 2013, we returned to London and started living together. The next nine months were amongst the most nurtured, loving, supported, joyful times in my life. Simultaneously it was also a very difficult time for me, because it came from a place of not knowing, of no commitment.

For me, not knowing is very difficult. I hate not knowing! I like to make decisions and come to conclusions and act, (yes, the left brain does still like to think it's in control although the right brain knows it's not!) But I had to accept that I could not control the outcome of our liaison. In fact I had no clue what the outcome would be. I did some work with one of my teachers about why not knowing is so painful for me. The real lesson for me is about **accepting** that I am not in charge of the outcome to many situations that I meet in my life. It's also seeing that not being in control or not being able to fix a situation is **not** the same as being pathetic (the initial judgement that my language based left brain jumps to.) The mantras or affirmations that I came away from that session with were:

'I powerfully step into being stuck, not in charge, in a place of not knowing.'

'I can enjoy the present situation knowing I cannot affect the outcome.'

This is the most fundamental nature of surrender.

Each day that George stayed was a gift and was a choice, by both of us. For him to stay and for me to allow that. This letting-go of knowing on my part then gave George the freedom to make his choice. At the same time it really forced me to reflect on my own issues of neediness and commitment. I could see the immense gifts we were giving each other. I wanted that magical time to continue, but I also truly felt that if he decided to leave it would be with my blessing, to fulfill his dream of having a family. I knew that whatever happened in the future, I would have no regrets about the time we were spending together, as I would always carry the gifts and the lessons with me.

This is the most fundamental nature of acceptance.

I am always surprised when people want to hold on to someone that has clearly stated they don't want to be in the relationship any more. If we love someone, surely we want them to be happy, not keep them prisoner? And contrary to the intention, grasping often pushes the other person away rather than pulling them closer.

It is interesting to observe how many people object even to this philosophy of freedom of choice. So often our own egos seem to come before the best interests of the people that we profess to love, leading to relationships based on co-dependency, fear of rejection and insecurity, rather than love and blessings for the other.

At the end of *Corporate Bitch to Shaman* I talk about coming to a place of surrender and setting the intention of each day to be to live with joy and to live as love. Those intentions help me to be in the moment day by day, without getting caught up in the past or in the future. If the moment is painful, acknowledge that pain and know that it will pass as all things pass. If the moment is joyful, appreciate it with gratitude and again know that it will pass. Life is a succession of moments and we can never re-live any of them. We have to be present as they occur or they are gone without us noticing them.

(Eckhart Tolle wrote an important book on this which turned into a best seller called the *Power of Now*[15]*)*. But it is easy for us to forget to be present when the ego lives in its attachments to the experiences of the past or its fear or hope regarding the future.

To complete bringing my personal story up to date, in September 2013, I took a group of clients to work with the shamans in Peru and on my return George asked me to marry him and to step into a soul contract of mutual nurture and evolution. That is the new journey that we have embarked on together. We accept our soul connection, the ability to nurture each other and to help each other become more powerful and magnificent, but without neediness or dependency, with choice and freedom. If you can work like that within a relationship it is a fantastic gift to yourself and to the beloved. It's very close to my intention with my clients in therapy sessions too. I try to hold the temenos for them to be seen and heard, with unconditional love, without judgement or projection. I encourage them to face their wounding and transform their lives towards living their purpose and their potential in optimal health. So let's move on to the theory and practice of how and why this is possible, using a wide variety of body-mind and non-local techniques derived from millennia of experiences across a wide range of lineages.

---

[15] Tolle, Eckhart. 1999. *The Power of Now* USA: New World Library

Chapter 2: The Science of the Inforealm

'Should science be a fundamentalist belief-system? Or should it be based on open-minded enquiry into the unknown?

'In no other field of scientific endeavor do otherwise intelligent people feel free to make public claims based on prejudice and ignorance. No one would denounce research in physical chemistry, say, while knowing nothing about the subject. Yet in relation to psychic phenomena, committed materialists feel free to disregard the evidence and behave irrationally and unscientifically while claiming to speak in the name of science and reason. They abuse the authority of science and bring rationalism into disrepute.'[16] (Rupert Sheldrake)

I have never met Dr. Larry Dossey of the United States, but I am indebted to his pioneering work and, with his approval, I have cast *Temenos Touch* in his framework of Eras of Healing. Almost all psychotherapy and a lot of complementary therapy seems to lie firmly in what he defines as Era II, the world of the body-mind, which is gradually being acknowledged and accepted by most medical practitioners. But shamanic and energy healing tend to move into what he defines as Era III, and work there is often still perceived as spiritual rather than scientific. In this book I want to address this misconception.

Dossey served as a battalion surgeon in Vietnam, where he was decorated for valour. He went on to help establish the Dallas Diagnostic Association and was Chief of Staff of Medical City Dallas Hospital in 1982. In 1989 he released his

[16] Sheldrake, Rupert. 2013. *The Science Delusion* p.257 London, UK: Coronet, Hodder & Stoughton Ltd.

paradigm-altering book, *Recovering the Soul*,[17] and since then he has been invited to lecture at major medical schools and hospitals around the world, focusing on the 'non-local mind', that is mind unconfined to the brain and body, spread infinitely throughout space and time.

He defines three distinct types or 'Eras' of healing methodology.[18]

- Era I believes all forms of therapy are physical and the body is regarded as a mechanism that functions according to deterministic principles. This encompasses most of modern Western medical technology. Mind or consciousness is equated with the functioning of the brain.
- Era II describes the mind-to-body medical approaches that involve the psychosomatic effects of one's consciousness on one's own body, i.e. what you think affects your health. But mind is still seen as a function of brain chemistry and anatomy. These therapies include psychosomatic medicine, biofeedback, hypnosis, meditation etc.
- Era III sees mind as unconfined by either space or time: it is boundless and unlimited. It is recognised that our non-local mind may affect healing both within and between people. Non-contact healing modalities between people in each others' presence, as well as between people distant from each other, become possible with non-local mind, as do healings backwards and forwards in time.

Some of the work I do these days and the techniques I describe in this book are firmly in Era II, the body-mind. This is our internal power, our potential: including the power of the placebo effect if you want to think of it that way. Other parts of the work I do and describe here are firmly in Era III, the world of non-locality.

Before turning to the healing methods themselves, I want

---

[17] Dossey, Larry, M.D. 1989. *Recovering the Soul: A Scientific and Spiritual Search* Bantam Doubleday Dell Publishing Group
[18] http://www.dossey.com/larry/QnA.html

to share my understanding of the concept of non-locality and how we can start to explain it and then use it.

The concept of non-locality originally came from quantum physics and actually it's not that new, which makes it even more surprising that we don't all know about it and it's not more widely taught in schools. The concept has been around since at least 1935 when Albert Einstein, the father of general relativity theory, denounced quantum physics as a flawed theory because its mathematical underpinning inferred bizarre and nonsensical concepts such as '*spooky action at a distance*',[19] whereby particles were somehow entangled, allowing them to communicate instantaneously with each other over vast distances. This contradicted Einstein's theory that nothing could travel faster than the speed of light, hence he concluded that quantum physics had to be wrong.

Over the past several decades, some of the most technologically advanced experiments conducted in linear accelerators have proved Einstein wrong and quantum physics correct.

The experiment which finally resolved the theoretical argument about the existence of non-locality was one in which two quanta of light, known as twin photons because they were ejected from a single source at the speed of light in opposite directions, were demonstrated to maintain their connection to one another, no matter how far apart they were.

For example, if scientists changed the polarisation (direction of spin) of one of the photons, the polarisation of the other **instantaneously** changed at its distant measurement site. This demonstrated that the twins must be connected in some way, but how did each of them instantaneously know what the other was doing? If nothing can travel faster than the speed of light, as postulated by

---

[19] Letter from Einstein to Max Born, 3 March 1947; *The Born-Einstein Letters; Correspondence between Albert Einstein and Max and Hedwig Born from 1916 to 1955*, Walker, New York, 1971. (cited in M. P. Hobson; et al. *Quantum Entanglement and Communication Complexity (1998)*. pp 1/13.)

Einstein and at the core of physics for the last century, the measured result should be impossible. Something else must be travelling faster than light to instantaneously alert the second twin of a change in the first one. This is the concept of non-local correlation.

Although it was in the world of quantum physics that non-locality was first theoretically postulated and then experimentally proven, in the twenty-first century non-locality is cropping up in many disciplines including cosmology, evolutionary biology, medicine (particularly associated with dying and near death patients) and consciousness research. In technical terms that I am not going to go into in detail here, but which are important for the physicists' explanation of the inforealm that I am working to introduce, it is not just that non-local events are simultaneously correlated or connected, they also appear to be coherent. Very briefly, to be coherent, waves must be of the same amplitude (size), and of the same frequency (in phase in time), with a constant spatial phase difference.

Much of my recent understanding and knowledge about the rapidly expanding mountain of academic evidence for non-local, correlated and coherent effects comes from Ervin Laszlo. He has held positions as a professor of philosophy, systems theory and futures studies in the USA, Europe and the Far East. He is founder and president of the international think-tank the Club of Budapest and also of the General Evolution Research Group. He has spent more than forty years searching for an 'integral theory of everything', searching for meaning through science. In that process he has written seventy-five books, which have been translated into twenty languages. His words in many cases seem more authentic and authoritative than any I could write on this topic, as befitting a man who has dedicated so much of his life to this research.

For interested readers I highly recommend *The Akashic Experience: Science and the Cosmic Memory Field*, a compilation in which Laszlo has pulled together experiences and explanations of non-locality from twenty leading authorities in fields such as psychiatry, physics, philosophy, anthropology, natural healing, near-death experience and spirituality.

In his own work, *Science and the Akashic Field: An Integral Theory of Everything* Laszlo writes, *'it is clear that nonlocal coherence has important implications. It signals that there is not only matter and energy in the universe, but also a more subtle yet real element: an element that connects, and which produces the observed quasi-instant forms of coherence.*

'Identifying this connecting element could solve the puzzles at the forefront of scientific research and point the way toward a more fertile paradigm.' [20]

In *Corporate Bitch to Shaman* I introduced the concept of the holographic universe, based on the work of Professor of physics, David Bohm, and his ground-breaking book *Wholeness and the Implicate Order.*[21] This was one of the earliest explanations of the entangled universe, using the metaphor of a hologram. One of the amazing features of a hologram is that if you smash it into a million tiny pieces, each piece contains not just a part of the picture, but the whole picture, from a different perspective. Bohm proposed that each region of the universe, from the macrocosmic to the microcosmic, contains the total structure enfolded within it. Each region of space-time contains information about every other point in space-time. Since Bohm's initial proposition the holographic universe has been given a number of alternative names by a range of physicists including holofield, implicate order or hyperspace.

Over the years Laszlo initially named this implicate order, the deeper dimension of the universe which is enfolded in the explicate order (the normal, large scale, three dimensional world), the QVI (Quantum Vacuum Interaction) field, then the psi-field. Most recently he labels it the Akashic or A-field

---

[20] Laszlo, Ervin. 2007. *Science and the Akashic Field: An Integral Theory of Everything (Second Edition)* pp60-61 Rochester, Vermont, USA: Inner Traditions

[21] Bohm, David. 1980. *Wholeness and the Implicate Order* UK: Routledge & Paul Kegan

in honour of the ancient Sanskrit concept of Akasha, meaning space.

He concludes *'Beyond the puzzle-filled world of the mainstream sciences, a new concept of the universe is emerging. The established concept is transcended; in its place comes the in-formed universe, rooted in the rediscovery of ancient tradition's Akashic Field as the vacuum-based holofield.*

'In this concept the universe is a highly integrated, coherent system: a 'supermacroscopic quantum system'. Its crucial feature is in-formation that is generated, conserved, and conveyed, and links all its parts…

'Thanks to in-formation conserved and conveyed by the A-field, the universe is of mind-boggling coherence. All that happens in one place happens also in other places; all that happened at one time happens also at all times after that. Nothing is 'local', limited to where and when it is happening. All things are global, indeed cosmic, for all things are connected, and the memory of all things extends to all places and to all times.

'This is the concept of the in-formed universe, the view of the world that will hallmark science and society in the coming decades.'[22] (emphasis added).

Rupert Sheldrake is another controversial visionary who has come to a similar conclusion, although his doctorate is in biochemistry and he worked as a cell biologist and plant physiologist before turning to parapsychology, hence he approached the problem from a biological, evolutionary perspective and uses different terminology. In *The Science Delusion*[23] he starts out by listing ten core beliefs that he perceives many scientists take for granted, without questioning their veracity and hence without questioning the conclusions drawn from using them as assumptions. These include the following:

- *'Everything is essentially mechanical…*

---

[22] Laszlo, Ervin. 2007. *Science and the Akashic Field: An Integral Theory of Everything (Second Edition)* p.80 Rochester, Vermont, USA: Inner Traditions

[23] Sheldrake, Rupert. 2013. *The Science Delusion* London, UK: Coronet, Hodder & Stoughton Ltd.

- *All matter is unconscious. It has no inner life or subjectivity or point of view. Even human consciousness is an illusion produced by the material activities of brains...*
- *Minds are inside heads and are nothing but the activities of brains...*
- *Memories are stored as material traces in brains and are wiped out at death.'*[24]

Chapter by chapter Sheldrake goes on to bust these often still prevailing myths in terms of the findings of modern science. But despite the mounting evidence against any rationality for these beliefs, they still do hold sway in much of society. As an Era III healer (and to a lesser extent Era II healer also), I am working outside these beliefs in all that I do, which is why the more scientific and experiential evidence I can bring to bear to reach out to those whose minds are not totally closed to change, the better.

Sheldrake introduces what he calls morphic fields, within and around self-organising systems, which organise the characteristic structures and patterns of activity inside those systems. According to his theory, morphic fields contain an inherent memory transmitted from previous similar systems by morphic resonance and over time these fields tend to become increasingly habitual.

In a condensed form he summarises his theory as follows:

- *'Self-organising systems including molecules, cells, tissues, organs, organisms, societies and minds are made up of nested hierarchies or holarchies of holons or morphic units.*
- *The wholeness of each level depends on an organising field, called a morphic field. This field is within and around the system it organises, and is a vibratory pattern of activity that interacts with electromagnetic and quantum fields of the system.*
- *Morphic fields are shaped by morphic resonance from all similar past systems, and thus contain a cumulative collective memory. Morphic resonance depends on similarity, and is not attenuated by distance in space or time. Morphic fields are local, within and*

---

[24] Sheldrake, Rupert. 2013. *The Science Delusion* pp7-8 London, UK: Coronet, Hodder & Stoughton Ltd.

around the systems they organise, but morphic resonance is non-local.

- *Morphic resonance involves a transfer of form or in-form-ation rather than a transfer of energy.*
- *Morphic fields are fields of probability, like quantum fields, and they work by imposing patterns on otherwise random events in the systems under their influence.*
- *All self-organising systems are influenced by self-resonance from their own past, which plays an essential role in maintaining a holon's identity and continuity.*'[25]

However, Sheldrake acknowledges that his hypothesis still doesn't address the underlying question of how morphic resonance works. He puts forward a couple of suggestions, including Bohn's implicate order, the zero-point energy field, '*Or maybe it depends on new kinds of physics as yet unthought of.*'[26]

That takes us back to the Akashic field of Ervin Laszlo who writes, '*The time has come to add another field to science's repertory of universal fields. Although fields, like other entities, are not to be multiplied beyond the scope of necessity, it seems evident that a further field is required to account for the special kind of coherence revealed at all scales and domains of nature, from the microdomain of quanta, through the mesodomain of life, to the macrodomain of the cosmos... Just as electric and magnetic effects are conveyed by the EM-field, attraction among massive objects by the G-field, and attraction and repulsion among the particles of the nucleus by quantum fields, so we must recognize that a universal in-formation field conveys the effect we described as 'nonlocal coherence' throughout the many domains of nature.*'[27]

Laszlo is very clear that from a scientist's perspective, non-local coherence is now a proven phenomenon. It is a real, measurable, observable field that we can strive to

---

[25] Sheldrake, Rupert. 2013. *The Science Delusion* pp99-100 London, UK: Coronet, Hodder & Stoughton Ltd.

[26] Sheldrake, Rupert. 2013. *The Science Delusion* p.101 London, UK: Coronet, Hodder & Stoughton Ltd.

[27] Laszlo, Ervin. 2007. *Science and the Akashic Field: An Integral Theory of Everything (Second Edition)* p.75 Rochester, Vermont, USA: Inner Traditions

understand and then use. This does not require or imply any sort of divine being or spiritual attribution.

To me, accessing this comprehensive 'in-formation' field outside the normal reality of linear time and space, is exactly the intention and function of altered states of consciousness, including out of body experiences, remote viewing, shamanic journeying, hallucinogenic experiences and meditation. As I step into the space of Era III healing I am trying to get into a brain-wave state that allows me to access this 'in-formation' field. Metaphorically I have to become the right light source to read the hologram, which means sending out the right waves to access the holographic universe or inforealm.

This is not a special skill however. We are all capable of doing this if we choose to. Many of the exercises I describe in this book are some of the techniques that practitioners use to do this, but there are a great many others. The key to the paradigm shift is accepting that it is possible. As Laszlo says, *'The recognition that the Akashic experience is a real and fundamental part of human experience has unparalleled importance for our time. When more people grasp the fact that they can have, and are perhaps already having, Akashic experiences, they will open their mind to them, and the experiences will occur more and more frequently, and to more and more people. A more evolved consciousness will spread in the world.'*[28]

---

[28] Laszlo, Ervin. 2009. *The Akashic Experience: Science and the Cosmic Memory Field* p.7 Rochester, Vermont, USA: Inner Traditions

Chapter 3: Neurobiology of the Body-mind, Stress and Trauma

'If frightening sensations… are not given the time and attention needed to move through the body and resolve/dissolve (as in trembling and shaking), the individual will continue to be gripped by fear and other negative emotions. The stage is set for a trajectory of mercurial symptoms. Tension in the neck, shoulders and back will likely evolve over time to the syndrome of fibromyalgia. Migraines are also common somatic expressions of unresolved stress. The knots in the gut may mutate to common conditions like irritable bowel syndrome, severe PMS or other gastrointestinal problems such as spastic colon. These conditions deplete the energy resources of the sufferer and may take the form of chronic fatigue syndrome. These sufferers are most often the patients with cascading symptoms who visit doctor after doctor in search of relief, and generally find little help for what ails them. Trauma is the great masquerader and participant in many maladies and 'dis-eases' that afflict sufferers. ***It can perhaps be conjectured that unresolved trauma is responsible for a majority of the illnesses of modern mankind.'***[29] (Emphasis added) (Peter Levine)

In the last Chapter I introduced non-locality and the science underlying Era III healing. Now in this Chapter and the next, I want to take a step back and look at the modern neurobiology that is increasingly demonstrating the validity of Era II healing and the body-mind approaches to therapy. In Chapter 5 I will move on to theories of the holonomic brain

[29] Levine, Peter A. PhD. 2010. *In An Unspoken Voice: How the Body Releases Trauma and Restores Goodness* p.184 Berkeley, California, USA: North Atlantic Books

that allow interaction of the neurobiological brain with the inforealm and hence link Era II and Era III healing.

Psychoneuroimmunology

Dr. Candace Pert was one of the pioneers of the field of psychoneuroimmunology (PNI) that has developed since the 1970s. PNI is the area of medical research that investigates the physiological connections between our thoughts (psyche), our nervous system (neurology) and our immune system. It has demonstrated unequivocally that what we think affects our health. Initially Pert was ostracised for her insights, but later she was re-embraced by the established medical community. She served as Chief of the Section on Brain Biochemistry in the Clinical Neuroscience Branch of the National Institute of Mental Health (NIMH), held a Research Professorship in the Department of Physiology and Biophysics at Georgetown University School of Medicine in Washington, DC and helped to found RAPID Laboratories, Inc.

In a nutshell, PNI has demonstrated that '*the three classically separated areas of neuroscience, endocrinology, and immunology, with their various organs – the brain; the glands; and the spleen, bone marrow, and lymph nodes – are actually joined to each other in a multidirectional network of communication, linked by information carriers known as neuropeptides.*'[30]

The neuropeptide ligands and other information carrying chemicals which travel throughout the body lead to the emotions such as hunger, anger, pain, relaxation and sexual drive, therefore '*what we experience as an emotion or a feeling is also a mechanism for activating a particular neuronal circuit – simultaneously throughout the brain and body – which generates a behaviour involving the whole creature, with all the necessary physiological changes that behaviour would require.*'[31] This is the

---

[30] Pert Ph.D., Candace B. 1999. *Molecules of Emotion, Why You Feel the Way You Feel* p.184 London, U.K.: Simon & Schuster
[31] Pert Ph.D., Candace B. 1999. *Molecules of Emotion, Why You Feel the Way You Feel* p.145 London, U.K.: Simon & Schuster

physiological explanation of the interconnectedness between all that we feel emotionally and how our physical bodies react throughout every cell. This is the first stage of recognising that our mental, emotional and physical health all go hand-in-hand.

I would hope that for many of you reading this, it does not seem surprising. It might even seem obvious! But even today sickness in the body is frequently treated without enquiring about how we are feeling emotionally, or how our lives are going. Are we happy or depressed? Are we lonely or in a relationship? If the latter, is it nurturing or abusive? Does our work make us feel stressed or fulfilled? The person needs to be treated holistically, not just as a physical machine, as Era II medical research clearly demonstrates.

Within the brain, it is in the limbic brain, particularly the amygdala, that the intense emotions take place.

It is the dorsolateral prefrontal cortex that connects us to the outside world and the endpoint of the dorsal pathway tells the brain how to interact with external stimuli.

The medial prefrontal cortex is in direct communication with muscles, joints and visceral organs and registers their sensations into consciousness.

The prefrontal cortex and the limbic system together relay messages to the hypothalamus, which connects the brain to the endocrine system, responsible for releasing all the different sorts of neuropeptides and hormones into the body. These are the organs responsible for physical and emotional ease or 'dis-ease'.

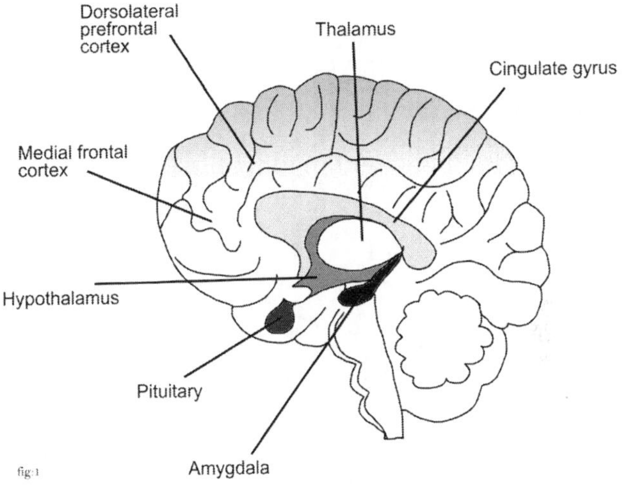

fig:1

Stress and hyper-arousal

One extremely common mental problem (dis-ease) these days that has a massive impact on the lives of many people, is stress. It has been extensively researched that when people feel under stress it results in a major inhibition of neuropeptide flow, which in turn leads to a suppression of the active functioning of the immune system, which in turn upsets the body's normal healing response.

In other words, mental and emotional stress makes us physically ill.

This occurs because there are two interconnected protection systems in the body, one for external threats and one for internal threats. The hypothalamus-pituitary-adrenal axis (HPA axis) is responsible for responding to external threat. The immune system is responsible for responding to internal threat.

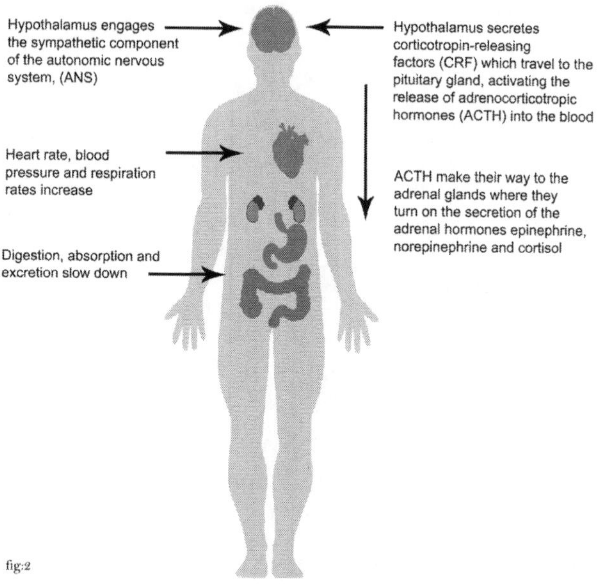

fig:2

In response to perceptions of stress registered in the brain (an external threat), the hypothalamus secretes corticotropin-releasing factors (CRF) which travel to the pituitary gland, activating the release of adrenocorticotropic hormones (ACTH) into the blood. The ACTH make their way to the adrenal glands where they are the signal to turn on the secretion of the adrenal hormones epinephrine, norepinephrine and cortisol.

Adrenal stress hormones constrict the blood vessels in the forebrain (responsible for executive reasoning and the conscious mind) reducing its ability to engage in conscious volitional action and redirecting vascular flow to the hindbrain (the source of reflex activity and the unconscious mind). This makes sense for survival because in an emergency, the faster the information processing for reflex reactions, the more likely it is that the organism will survive.

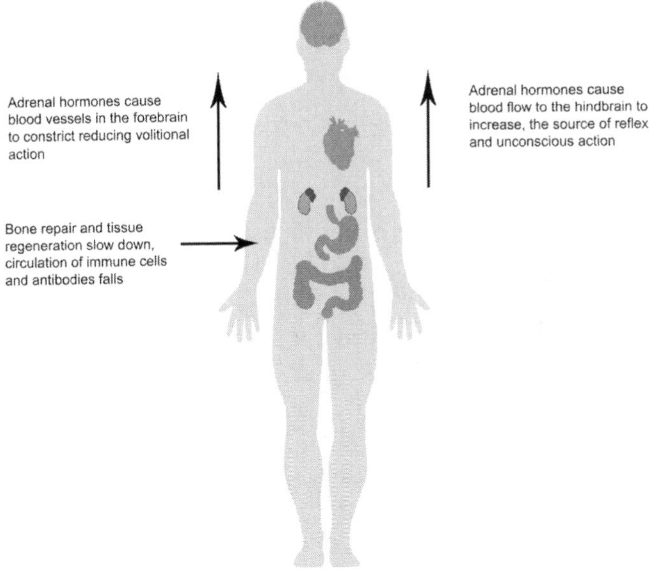

fig:3 The body is mobilized for fight or flight with dissociated rage and panic

The stress hormones also directly increase our heart rate, trigger the release of glucose from energy stores, constrict the blood vessels of the digestive tract and increase the flow of blood to our skeletal muscle getting them all ready for fight or flight. But once the alarm to release these stress hormones has sounded and our body has become mobilised for action, there has to be a physical release. Otherwise the levels of these stress hormones build up in the blood, wreaking havoc on the second protection system, the immune system, which protects us from internal threats such as bacteria and viruses.

In particular when we are making cortisol, the visceral organs stop doing their work of digestion, absorption, excretion and other functions that provide for the repair and replacement of cells and the production of the body's energy reserves. Bone repair and wound healing are slowed and levels of circulating immune cells and antibodies fall. In high levels cortisol kills our brain cells. Cortisol has been shown to reduce muscle mass, increase bone loss and osteoporosis, increase blood pressure, interfere with the generation of new skin cells, lower immune function and reduce memory and learning abilities.

So the external protection system is useful when there is a genuine threat to our survival, but it was never designed to be kept in the 'on' position for prolonged periods of time. While it is kept on, the internal protection system is turned down to low.

The trouble is that in today's world many of us are constantly worried. This results in chronically elevated stress hormones that we don't release through fight or flight and with the immune system turned down, of course this makes us prone to sickness.

The first and best possible solution is to try to change our lives to reduce our stress levels and the illness that accompanies high stress. However people often don't see that as being possible.

The second possible action is to deal with stress differently when it arises. No matter where or how we live, we can be sure that at times stressful situations will arise in life. Things are constantly changing and we cannot really control what happens out there. All we **can** control is how we react to events internally, not what others do and say or what happens in the world around us. How we react of course does then ripple through onto others and onto the reality we create for ourselves, as well as directly onto our own health or 'dis-ease'.

An example is to imagine you are standing waiting for a train in the morning. It's late. Maybe some depressed person has thrown themselves onto the track. You can see the people on the platform around you having a variety of different responses. At one end of the spectrum you can choose to allow your blood pressure to rise and anger and stress hormones to flood your system. 'The stupid train is late. I'm going to miss my meeting. How could anyone do that in the rush hour. Stupid person. I'm so irritated. Aaarrrggghhhh.' At the other end of the spectrum you can choose to put out sympathy for the poor person that has just died and their family and friends. You can choose to give thanks for your own health and wellbeing and you can take the extra time to read your book, or talk to the person you are with, or enjoy the sun on the platform. You allow peaceful, relaxing hormones to enter the system and you fill your body with gratitude. Most importantly, you acknowledge that you have the power of choice. It is up to you to choose how you react to life's big and little events.

In both scenarios, you don't change what time the train finally turns up.

In both scenarios, you don't influence what time you get to your appointment.

But in the first case you enter your destination full of anger and stress and probably lash out at everyone in irritation. In the second case you enter the room calmly, in a state of compassion and gratitude and you tell everyone how pleased you are to be with them today, although you are sorry for any inconvenience you have caused them by being late. That reaction is what goes on to create your environment for the rest of the day, because people then go on to react to your action and treat you in a different way depending on your initial greeting, allowing either the anger and stress or the love and gratitude to snowball, with a corresponding neuropeptide and hormonal response in the physical body. You create health or 'dis-ease'. Mentally, physically and emotionally.

The third possible choice is that once we have experienced stress, we can consciously act to release it. There are many proven techniques that we can engage in that interact with the endocrine system and the nervous system in a positive way to reduce the impact of stress on the body. These include meditation, breathing techniques, (known in yogic practices as pranayama) and movement practices such as kundalini yoga, shamanic dance, five rhythms and ecstatic dance. Many of these allow the body to express itself freely. Why this expression is necessary for healing is explained within the next section on trauma.

Trauma and hypo-arousal (dissociation)

Trauma is at the extreme end of stress and arises when a situation is overwhelming and the person involved feels helpless. They fear they will not survive and the initial fight or flight responses to a threat are impossible, or have failed.

Franz Ruppert is one of the leading psychotherapists specialising in trauma therapy. He presents a model where trauma results in a psychological split of the psyche into three parts: the traumatised self, the survival self and the healthy self.

The healthy self aspires to integration and wholeness. The survival self does everything it can to keep the traumatised part safe, which may mean refusing to look at or acknowledge the trauma, which is suppressed into the unconscious. The survival self creates a way of living which does help us to continue living, but it also keeps our psyche split and stuck in the old belief system.

In this model the healthy self and the survival self will always be in conflict: one wants to look at the pain in order for the psyche to be healed and integrated and the other wants to suppress the pain, to avoid feeling the trauma.

As Ruppert puts it '*Attempts to bring these trauma symptoms under control without establishing the connection with the original trauma event cannot logically lead to any permanent success. The effect of an unconsidered suppression of trauma energies is more likely to exacerbate the situation for the person concerned.*'[32]

---

[32] Ruppert, Franz. 2012. *Symbiosis & Autonomy, Symbiotic Trauma and Love Beyond Entanglements* pp172-173 Steyning, UK: Green Balloon Publishing

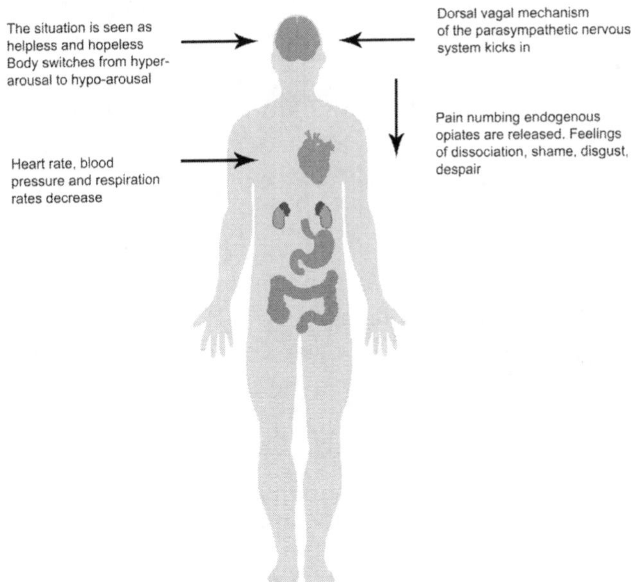

fig:4

Dr. Peter Levine gives a graphic explanation of the physiology of the freezing that takes place in the physical body in response to extremes of fear. *'In addition to the well-known fight and flight reactions, there is a third, lesser-known reaction to threat: immobilisation. Ethologists call this 'default' state of paralysis tonic immobility (TI)… It occurs when active responses are not likely to be effective in escaping or removing the source of threat… Trauma occurs when we are intensely frightened and are either physically restrained or perceive that we are trapped. We freeze in paralysis and/or collapse in overwhelming helplessness…*

'In freezing, your muscles stiffen against a mortal blow, and you feel 'scared stiff'. On the other hand, when you experience death as being unequivocally imminent… your muscles collapse as though they have lost all their energy. In this 'default' reaction (when it has become chronic, as it does in trauma), you feel that you are in a state of helpless resignation and lack the energy to fuel your life and move forward. This collapse, defeat and loss of the will to live are at the very core of deep trauma…

'A fourth biological function of immobility is that it triggers a profoundly altered state of numbing. In this state, extreme pain and terror are dulled… This 'humane' analgesic effect is mediated by the flooding of endorphins, the body's own profound morphine pain-relief system… In this state of analgesia, the victim may witness the event as through from outside his or her body, as if it were happening to someone else… Such distancing, called dissociation, helps to make the unbearable bearable.'[33]

In the animal kingdom Levine observed that wild animals often tremble when they are stressed or confined or when they are able to get up after a state of tonic immobility. And when human beings are allowed to express from the body, they frequently shake when they are cold, anxious, angry or fearful. Patients sometimes shake uncontrollably as they awake from anesthesia. In Qigong and Kundalini yoga ecstatic and blissful states are often accompanied by shaking and trembling. And in movement meditations the body is encouraged to express itself fully, whether that is sadness, anger or fear or indeed love, joy or a desire for comforting physical touch from another human being.

Levine observes that all these tremblings are the natural way that our bodies release and shake off the damaging hormones released in response to the external threat protection mechanism. They are part of our homeostatic balancing ability. However, these tremblings are often suppressed in modern life and when the high threat hormones are not allowed to be released from the system, we enter a state of constant anxiety and disease, leading to the prevalence of PTSD, illness and disconnection from society.

Why meditation helps to alleviate stress

Even when we are not facing situations that might be defined as trauma, there is a great deal of evidence to suggest that as a regular practice, meditation is one of the best ways to

---

[33] Levine, Peter A. PhD. 2010. *In An Unspoken Voice: How the Body Releases Trauma and Restores Goodness* pp48-50 Berkeley, California, USA: North Atlantic Books

release day to day stress from the system.

Dr. Dharma Singh Khalsa is President and Medical Director of the Alzheimer's Prevention Foundation in Tucson, Arizona. He is also a yogi and conducts workshops on brain longevity and Medical Meditation. In *Meditation as Medicine*, he reports the conclusions of studies by the US Federal Government's Office of Alternative Medicine on meditation and Dr. Herbert Benson of the Harvard Medical School including:

'Meditation creates a unique hypometabolic state, in which the metabolism is in an even deeper state of rest than during sleep.

'Meditation is the only activity that reduces blood lactate, a marker of stress and anxiety.

'The calming hormones melatonin and serotonin are increased by meditation, and the stress hormone cortisol is decreased.

'Meditation has a profound effect upon three key indicators of ageing: hearing ability, blood pressure, and vision of close objects.

'Long-term meditators experience 80 percent less heart disease and 50 percent less cancer than non-meditators.'[34]

[34] Singh Khalsa, M.D., Dharma and Stauth, Cameron. 2001. *Meditation as Medicine* p.8 New York, NY, USA: Fireside

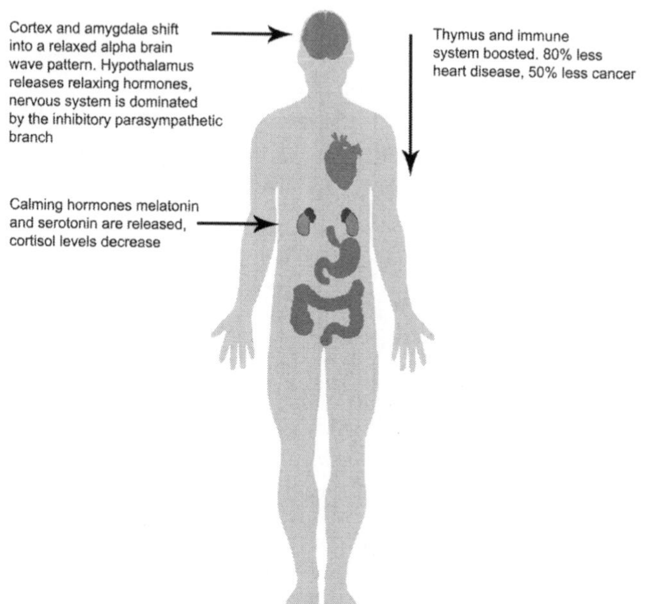

fig:5

Ideal condition for healing

Singh Khalsa explains that this works because when a person meditates, the cortex and the amygdala shift into a relaxed alpha brain wave pattern. They send a message to the hypothalamus to release relaxing hormones, whilst the nervous system is dominated by the inhibitory parasympathetic branch. This in turn favours the organs and glands of immunity, such as the thymus, producing the ideal condition for healing.

In addition, the ancient Sanskrit mantras which are often chanted to accompany meditation have the very specific physiological action of vibrating the upper palate of the mouth, which connects upwards to the pituitary gland, thereby altering its secretions into the endocrine system. The vibrations arising from these mantras can also stimulate the hypothalamus and the vagus nerve which travels through the neck and services the heart, lungs, intestinal tract and back muscles.

All this scientific and medical evidence underpins why Era II healing is essential. The mind and body are as one and to allow clients to return to good mental and emotional health, we must work with the stress and trauma that are held in the physical body, not just the mind, because it is the bodily experience of stress that make us sick and the bodily experiences during trauma that get triggered and re-enacted – often inappropriately, in post traumatic stress disorder.

Through observation and awareness of how different sensations in the muscles, joints and visceral organs of the body make us feel emotionally, the medial prefrontal cortex can gradually modify the response of the amygdala to external stimuli. However this needs to be done in a safe, held space, for the survival self to allow the healthy self to dare to feel the trauma.

As Levine describes it, '*In order to unravel this tangle of fear and paralysis, we must be able to voluntarily contact and experience those frightening physical sensations; we must be able to confront them long enough for them to shift and change. To resist the immediate defensive ploy of avoidance, the most potent strategy is to move toward the fear, to contact the immobility itself and to consciously explore the various sensations, textures, images and thoughts associated with any discomfort that may arise.*'[35]

And from years of experience, Levine **is** optimistic that body work is capable of providing a solution, sometimes very quickly. '*It is also possible to eliminate, sometimes instantaneously, psychosomatic, emotional and psychological symptoms that may have plagued you for decades.*'[36]

There is a debate in the psychotherapeutic community about whether **everyone** is suffering from trauma to some extent. I personally don't believe I have ever faced the life-threatening situation used in my definition of trauma above.

---

[35] Levine, Peter A. PhD. 2010. *In An Unspoken Voice: How the Body Releases Trauma and Restores Goodness* p.74 Berkeley, California, USA: North Atlantic Books

[36] Levine, Peter A. PhD. 2010. *In An Unspoken Voice: How the Body Releases Trauma and Restores Goodness* p.300 Berkeley, California, USA: North Atlantic Books

One of my teachers did suggest this was just a very efficient survival part in my psyche. That's not what I feel at this time, but maybe they're right!

Whether it is ubiquitous or not, trauma is certainly extremely common. Perhaps bizarrely, some of the most obvious causes of trauma like war and torture appear to be easier for people to release, because although horrific, they come from outside the system and have fewer personal, hidden feelings of shame or guilt associated with them. Next come other external events like accident or attack by someone outside the community or tribe. The source of the hardest traumas to deal with is symbiotic entanglement within the family or tribe, because the perpetrators were supposed to be protectors.

Levine believes acknowledgement of the prevalence of traumatisation in society today could lead to a dramatic improvement in health, as illustrated in his statement quoted at the beginning of this Chapter. The first necessity is for the source of the illness to be correctly recognised and acknowledged. The second is for this trauma to be released in an environment that feels safe for the individual and allows them to do the necessary body work as well as well as the mind work.

Chapter 4: Limbic Resonance, Attractor Pathways and Mirroring

'*The prevailing medical paradigm has no capacity to incorporate the concept that a relationship is a physiologic process, as real and as potent as any pill or surgical procedure.*'[37] (Thomas Lewis, Fari Aminin and Richard Lannon)

The symbiosis between mind and body means that, as well as working within our bodies for holistic Era II health of the mind, we must work with the neurological blockages in the brain, our mind-set, to reach our optimal health potential in the body.

Vast amounts of recent neurobiological research have started to reveal how the brain functions, helping to explain why we get stuck in certain emotional patterns, the conditioning and limiting beliefs of the past, and why we find it so difficult to release and step beyond these. Neurobiology is affirming Carl Jung's concept that 'perception is projection', that we see what we believe, not that we believe what we see.

A General Theory of Love[38], published in 2000, was one of the first academic psychiatric acknowledgements of the link between what we have experienced in the past and what we are able to feel and see in the present. It presents an array of evidence based on the neurobiology of the brain,

---

[37] Lewis, Thomas, M.D., Aminin, Fari, M.D., Lannon, Richard, M.D.. 2000. *A General Theory of Love* pp80-81 New York, USA: Vintage Books, Random House

[38] Lewis, Thomas, M.D., Aminin, Fari, M.D., Lannon, Richard, M.D.. 2000. *A General Theory of Love* New York, USA: Vintage Books, Random House

demonstrating that the experiences of the body and what we think we know or remember in the brain are not separate. This evidence depends on limbic resonance, regulation and revision.

The authors, Thomas Lewis M.D., Richard Lannon, M.D., and Fari Aminin, M.D. were all academic psychiatrists at the University of California San Francisco. They explain in detail the way that neurons in the brain learn and remember information through the creation of neural networks, which get stronger with use and wither when left unattended. The result is that *'In a neural network, new experiences blur the outlines of older ones. The reverse is also true: the neural past interferes with the present. Experience methodically rewires the brain and the nature of what it* ***has*** *seen dictates what it* ***can*** *see.'*[39]

In mathematical theory, an attractor is a state towards which the system tends to evolve regardless of the starting conditions of the system. In neurology, the pathways of recognition are called limbic attractors. When these are attractors exist the result is that *'A network then registers novel sensory information* ***as if it conformed to past experience.****'*[40]

This means that, *'Because human beings remember with neurons, we are disposed to see more of what we have already seen, hear anew what we have heard most often, think just what we have always thought. Our minds are burdened by an informational inertia whose headlong course is not easy to slow. As a life lengthens, momentum gathers.'*[41]

This leads to each of us creating our own version of what we believe to be the reality of any event or situation, because we all individually have different perceptions of that event or

---

[39] Lewis, Thomas, M.D., Aminin, Fari, M.D., Lannon, Richard, M.D.. 2000. *A General Theory of Love* p.135 New York, USA: Vintage Books, Random House

[40] Lewis, Thomas, M.D., Aminin, Fari, M.D., Lannon, Richard, M.D.. 2000. *A General Theory of Love* p.138 New York, USA: Vintage Books, Random House

[41] Lewis, Thomas, M.D., Aminin, Fari, M.D., Lannon, Richard, M.D.. 2000. *A General Theory of Love* p.141 New York, USA: Vintage Books, Random House

situation based on our unique past experiences and beliefs.

The limbic attractor pathways inside our brains also have a tendency to lead us to react to a new event in accordance with our existing beliefs, based on our previous experience. For example, if we have been told in the past that we are stupid, ugly or unable to do something, we are inclined to manipulate anyone telling us something new into the same old pattern and belief of inadequacy. We hear what we have projected a million times before, even though the information this time is different. We see what we have unconsciously decided we will see, even if that is not really what is there.

A huge amount of research is continuing in this area, focusing on neurobiology and the concept of neuroplasticity, which is the ability of the brain to change structurally and develop new neural connections that might allow us to escape the prison of the old limbic attractor pathways.

Myelin is an electrically insulating material that forms around the axons of some neurons in the brain and increases the speed at which impulses travel from cell to cell within the central nervous system. A new technology called diffusion tensor imaging allows observation of how these myelinated circuits remodel themselves during spatial learning and memory tasks. It has been observed that microstructural changes, that is neuroplasticity, can be seen after as little as two hours of training in a new task.

In *The Mindful Therapist*[42] Daniel J. Siegel M.D. defines three elements of brain, mind and relationship.

He defines brain as the extended nervous system distributed throughout the whole body, that is the physical mechanism of energy and information flow. (This is in accordance with the findings of psychoneuroimmunology.)

He defines mind as, in part, the way that this flow is regulated. He defines relationships as being the way energy and information flow is shared.

Siegel claims that the process of neuroplasticity involves at

---

[42] Siegel, Daniel J. M.D.. 2010. *The Mindful Therapist* New York, NY, USA: W.W.Norton & Company, Inc,

least three components:

- We are able to create and strengthen synaptic connections.
- We are able to stimulate new neurons to grow.
- We can increase myelinogenesis to enhance the conduction speed of neural electrical impulses.

He goes on to describe in his terminology how the mind which regulates the energetic flow has the capacity to change the extended nervous system of the brain because attention on the information flows leads to myelinogenesis. As a result, awareness has the power '*to focus attention in certain ways to shape the flow of energy and information. As this flow occurs, our mental regulation process drives the firing in the brain by initiating activity in specific patterns of neural connections that can then induce structural changes in the brain's connectivity.*'[43]

Just as in Levine's work **attending to the emotions** caused by particular sensations or movements of the body can rewire our reaction to those sensations, in Siegel's work **attending to the thoughts** caused by particular personal relationships and interactions can rewire our brain's reaction to those relationships.

This means we can escape the conditioning of our limbic attractors and consciously decide to change our reactions to events around us by rewiring our own brains through attention, also known as mindful awareness. The next question of course, is how to become mindfully aware? Siegel has a whole series of exercises that he has developed to enhance awareness, which are largely based on meditation techniques. Engaging in such mindful awareness is stepping into true self-responsibility, self-empowerment and choice.

This scientific work clearly does open the possibility of neurological change, of us being able to visualise a future different from our past, releasing the old limiting beliefs and conditioning. But it needs us to work to open these new neuronal pathways through new thinking, not sticking to the old attractor pathways formed by the old stories and patterns.

---

[43] Siegel, Daniel J. M.D.. 2010. *The Mindful Therapist* p.218 New York, NY, USA: W.W.Norton & Company, Inc..

We need to accept that those beliefs and patterns just might have been wrong and that there might be a different way of looking at things.

Since this work can be difficult, modern psychotherapy is focusing on the possibility of rewiring our brains through a relationship with an empathic other, receiving exogenous assistance to establish new limbic attractors. In the Journal of the American Medical Association, R.M. Glass concludes, *'Recent research in brain imaging, molecular biology, and neurogenetics has shown that psychotherapy changes brain function and structure. Such studies have shown that psychotherapy affects regional cerebral blood flow, neurotransmitter metabolism, gene expression, and persistent modifications in synaptic plasticity'.*[44]

Psychotherapy is also recognising that the most effective therapeutic relationship for changing our brain structure and function is not the left brain to left brain cognitive behavior therapy so in vogue in the early parts of the twenty-first century, but rather **affective** therapy involving right brain to right brain emotional connectivity between client and practitioner.

For twenty years Allan Schore has been at the forefront of promoting affective psychotherapy and his ideas are now becoming widely accepted and practised. He writes, *'Interdisciplinary data and updated clinical models lead me to conclude that the right hemisphere is dominant in treatment, and that psychotherapy is not the 'talking cure' but the affect communicating and regulating cure.'*[45]

Within the brain this process of change through relationship is possible partly because of the phenomenon known as mirroring, or resonance behaviour. Mirror neurons were initially observed in primates and fire both when an animal acts, and when it observes that same action being performed by another animal. So it doesn't matter whether

---

[44] Glass, R.M. (2008) Psychodynamic psychotherapy and research evidence. Bambi survives Godzilla? p.1589 *The Journal of the American Medical Association*, 300, 1587-1589.

[45] Schore, Allan N.. 2012. *The Science of the Art of Psychotherapy* p.85 New York, NY, USA: W.W. Norton & Company, Inc.

the animal is actually doing something or just watching it being done. These neurons are found in the premotor cortex and the insular cingulate, the areas of the brain that communicate internal bodily states and emotions. A number of neuroscientists have suggested that the mirror neuron system is central to empathy and intimacy.

As this research progresses, the power of the mirror neuron is being discovered to be greater than previously suspected. It has now been realised that it is not just what we actually **do**, what we **observe** and those we interact with that trigger these neurons, but also what we **imagine**.

Iain McGilchrist is a former Consultant Psychiatrist and Clinical Director at the Bethlem Royal & Maudsley Hospital, London. He is a major researcher in the field of brain neurology and writes the following about how our mirror neurons impact us.

'We already know from the discovery of the existence of mirror neurons that when we imitate something that we can see, it is as if we are experiencing it. But it goes further than this. Mental representation, in the absence of direct visual or other stimulus - in other words, imagining – brings into play some of the same neurons that are involved in direct perception. It is clear from this that, even when we so much as imagine doing something, never mind actually imitate it, it is, at some level which is far from negligible, as if we are actually doing it ourselves. Imagining something, watching someone else do something, and doing it ourselves share important neural foundations.

'Imagination, then, is not a neutral projection of images on a screen. We need to be careful of our imagination, since what we imagine is in a sense what we are and who we become.'[46]

This again enhances the possibility of endogenously induced changes in our neural wiring, simply through imagination, as well as providing evidence for how an empathic therapist can provide exogenous assistance to help clients develop different neural attractors, to allow them to

---

[46] McGilchrist, Iain. 2009. *The Master and his Emissary: The Divided Brain and the Making of the Western World* p.250 New Haven and London: Yale University Press

change their perceptions of the world.

The modern literature on affective psychotherapy is also widening the perception of the empathic therapist to a concept that is talked about as resonance, without really defining how that actually comes about. For instance Emanuel Hammer describes his receptive state for reaching the affect by **resonating** moment-to-moment with the patent's unconscious nonverbal right brain. *'By being more open in this manner, to resonating to the patient, I find pictures forming in my creative zones; an image crystallizes, reflecting the patient's experience... An empathic channel appeared to be established which carried his state or emotion my way via a kind of affective 'wireless'.'*[47]

I will talk much more about client-therapist relationships later, but I want to flag up here how dangerous I perceive the approach of intending to change the neural networks of the client to be in line with those of the therapist can be.

One of the therapeutic aims of working with a client as stated by Lewis, Aminin and Lannon is to reprogramme the limbic attractors of the client in a way which leads to a change in the client's perception of the world and new events that they experience. So far, so good. They continue that the intention is for the client to start to mirror the hopefully healthy belief systems of the therapist. They write, *'if therapy **works,** it transforms a patient's limbic brain and his emotional landscape forever. The person of the therapist will determine the shape of the new world a patient is bound for; the configuration of **his** limbic Attractors fixes those of the other. Thus the urgent necessity for a therapist to get his emotional house in order. His patients are coming to stay, and they may have to live there for the rest of their lives.'*[48]

They believe that this revising of limbic attractors will take a minimum of three years, and continue *'Wouldn't it be fabulous if one could compress a course of limbic instruction from years*

---

[47] Hammer, Emanuel F.. 1990. *Reaching the Affect: Style in the Psychodynamic Therapies* pp.99-100 New York, USA: Jason Aronson, Inc.

[48] Lewis, Thomas, M.D., Aminin, Fari, M.D., Lannon, Richard, M.D.. 2000. *A General Theory of Love* p.187 New York, USA: Vintage Books, Random House

into weeks or even days? The tantalizing mirage of a short (and cheap) psychotherapy, a cool and inviting oasis, has lured many across the parched sands of impossibility. The architecture of the emotional mind makes effective, fast-food therapy as much a creature of myth as the unicorn.'[49]

Personally I find the stance of **intending** to reprogramme the limbic attractors of clients to **mirror** those of the therapist very worrying. There is a recognition that the therapist needs to have done as much of his own personal work as possible to be of the greatest service to the client, but how many therapists are good enough role models to be used as cloning material for their clients?

In a related but different critique, the assumption that it takes years for psychotherapy to be effective appears to risk putting the therapist in the place of rescuer within the well-known victim, perpetrator, rescuer triangle. I am indebted to one of my own teachers, Vivian Broughton, for pointing out that frequently clients who come seeking help are used to seeing themselves as victims – that is the role they have adopted, consciously or unconsciously, in their family or society (that is the limbic attractor they enter the room with). As a consequence, they may be seeking a therapist to be a rescuer. Many therapists may enjoy taking on this role, indeed that may be what has led them into their chosen profession, but if they step into that rescuer role, they risk keeping their clients as victims. They may not be reprogramming the client's limbic attractors, they may be reinforcing them!

So although I totally applaud that more and more of modern medicine and neuroscience are moving out of the old Era I paradigm into Era II, acknowledging the mind-body connections, there is a potential danger that in this process some of the advocates of Era II therapies assume that this is the new final frontier whilst continuing to sideline or even deprecate Era III possibilities. If leaders in the field of

---

[49] Lewis, Thomas, M.D., Aminin, Fari, M.D., Lannon, Richard, M.D.. 2000. *A General Theory of Love* p.188 New York, USA: Vintage Books, Random House

neurobiology and eventually the establishment come to believe that Era II mind-body healing is the new holy grail, then Era III healing continues to be dismissed in favour of a slow and incomplete half-way house.

The leap into Era III healing takes us back to the issue of whether the brain is the same as mind is the same as consciousness? If the answer is no, then it becomes possible to speed things up and work in a larger arena of consciousness than that held purely within the therapist-client dyad, because it becomes possible to download information instantaneously into the neurological brain from the greater consciousness via the holonomic brain, the subject of Chapter 5.

And just a word of caution, this is an area where we need to be very clear on semantics, as for some therapists conscious behaviour is simply equated with the rational, verbalised, cognitive factors associated with the left brain and the somatic nervous system, whilst unconscious behaviour is equated with the intuitive, emotional, experiential processes associated with the right brain and the autonomic nervous system. But this neurological definition of consciousness applied to behaviour is not the same as the wider concepts of consciousness that I am talking about in the rest of this book, particularly in the next chapter.

Chapter 5: The Holonomic Brain, Mind and Consciousness

'*Is consciousness a product of the brain? The only certainty here is that anyone who thinks they can answer this question with certainty has to be wrong. We have only our conceptions of consciousness and of the brain to go on; and the one thing we do know for certain is that everything we know of the brain is a product of consciousness. That is, scientifically speaking, far more certain than that consciousness itself is a product of the brain. It may be or it may not... We do not know if mind depends on matter, because everything we know about matter is itself a mental creation.*'[50] (Iain McGilchrist)

These words of wisdom come from Iain McGilchrist, an eminent scholar who has been searching for the links between the brain, the mind and consciousness for decades.

In the materialist doctrine, only matter is real, the mind is the same as the brain, and consciousness is nothing but brain activity. The fact that by their own logic they must be wrong, as McGilchrist points out above, doesn't seem to stop the materialists from declaring they know the truth!

The traditional alternative to materialism is dualism, the doctrine that minds and brains are different and in particular minds are immaterial whilst brains are material.

Sheldrake provides a third alternative, neither materialism or dualism, in terms of the morphogenic or Akashic field, or inforealm, as already discussed in Chapter 2. He writes, '*We need not stay stuck in this materialist-dualist contradiction. There is a way out: a field theory of minds. We are used to the fact that fields exist*

---

[50] McGilchrist, Iain. 2009. *The Master and his Emissary: The Divided Brain and the Making of the Western World* pp19-20 New Haven and London: Yale University Press

both within and outside material objects. The field of a magnet is inside it and also extends beyond its surface. The gravitational field of the earth is inside the earth and also stretches out far beyond it, keeping the moon in its orbit. The electromagnetic field of a mobile phone is both inside it and extends all around it… I suggest that the fields of minds are within brains and extend beyond them.'[51] This allows for minds and brains to be different, but both are real. They are both subsets of something larger than either.

This concept of a field theory of mind and consciousness is gradually gaining ground, with supporting evidence emerging from a variety of scientific disciplines. Here I present some of this evidence, drawing on the expertise and experience of a cardiac surgeon, a psychoneuroimmunologist, a neuroscientist, an anaesthetist and several quantum physicists.

Pim van Lommel is a Dutch cardiac surgeon. Since 1986 he has been conducting extensive surveys of the near-death experiences (NDEs) of patients who survived cardiac arrest after being declared 'brain dead'. Some of them retain very clear memories of what they experienced in their bodies during that time, and some retain very clear images of what happened to them in 'another realm' while they were physiologically declared to be dead.

The NDE experiences that van Lommel's patients report include out-of-body experiences, holographic life reviews, meeting with deceased relatives and conscious returns into their bodies. He and his colleagues who have carried out this work have been able to rule out physiological, psychological and pharmacological explanations for what their patients experience.

He writes, *'NDEs are transformational, causing profound changes of life-insight and loss of the fear of death. The content of an NDE and the effects on patients seems similar worldwide, across all*

[51] Sheldrake, Rupert. 2013. *The Science Delusion* pp213-214 London, UK: Coronet, Hodder & Stoughton Ltd.

cultures and all times.'[52]

Van Lommel's own suggested explanation which he has put forward in detail in his book, *Consciousness Beyond Life: The Science of the Near-Death Experience*[53], is *'a concept in which our whole and undivided consciousness with declarative memories finds its origin in, and is stored in, a nonlocal space as wave-fields of information. This nonlocal aspect of consciousness can be compared to gravitational fields, where only the physical effects can be measured, and the fields themselves are not directly demonstrable. In this concept the cortex only serves as a relay station for parts of these wave-fields of consciousness to be received into or as our waking consciousness. The latter belongs to our physical body...*

'The neuronal networks should be regarded as functioning as receivers and conveyors, not as retainers of consciousness and memories. In this concept, consciousness is not rooted in the measurable domain of physics, our manifest world. The wave aspect of our indestructible consciousness in nonlocal space is inherently incapable of being measured by physical means. However, the physical aspect of consciousness, which originates from the wave aspect of our consciousness, can be measured by means of neuro-imaging techniques like EEG, fMRI, and PET-scan.

'Based on my NDE research, I conclude that our waking consciousness, which we experience as our daily consciousness, is only a complementary aspect of our whole and infinite nonlocal consciousness. This consciousness is based on indestructible and constantly evolving fields of information, where all knowledge, wisdom, and unconditional love are present and available, and these fields of consciousness are stored in a dimension beyond our concept of time and space with nonlocal and universal interconnectedness.'[54]

---

[52] Van Lommel, Pim. Chapter 16 *Acceding to the Field: The Case of Near-Death Experiences in Survivors of Cardiac Arrest* p.178 in Laszlo, Ervin. 2009. *The Akashic Experience: Science and the Cosmic Memory Field* Rochester, Vermont, USA: Inner Traditions

[53] Van Lommel, Pim. 2011. *Consciousness Beyond Life: The Science of the Near-Death Experience* Harper One

[54] Van Lommel, Pim. Chapter 16 *Acceding to the Field: The Case of Near-Death Experiences in Survivors of Cardiac Arrest* pp191-192 in

This is a very clear description of consciousness as a field, in non-local space, with the brain serving only as a receiver of the waves of information which are stored outside the physical body.

Later on, after her original discoveries of the psychoneuroimmunological mind-body connections discussed in Chapter 3, Pert too came to believe that the neurological mind is simply the mechanism that connects the physical body with the external field where the information is stored, the inforealm. *'For me, God – a holy spirit, higher consciousness, or transcendent self – is found within the nonmaterial, nonlocal world that's the source of our mind, thoughts and emotions. I've called this the information realm, or 'inforealm', but it can also be called the field of infinite possibility, or the nonlocal or zero-point field. In this domain, which is everywhere and nowhere, we're all connected, all one.'*[55]

Neuroscientists have reached a similar conclusion in the external storage version of what is now called holonomic brain theory, named in honour of the work carried out by the neuroscientist Karl Pribram, partially in collaboration with the quantum physicist David Bohm.

Initially Pribram proposed a model in which the distributed memory that exists throughout the brain is likened to a holographic storage network. Dendrites are extensions of the cell body of the neurons in the brain, specialised in receiving and processing information. They branch out in complex patterns and form what is knows as the dendritic arbour. Memory is encoded in a pattern in the brain created by the interference of waves from the electric oscillations originating in these synaptodendritic webs.[56] In an optical hologram, if you smash the hologram into a million

---

Laszlo, Ervin. 2009. *The Akashic Experience: Science and the Cosmic Memory Field* Rochester, Vermont, USA: Inner Traditions

[55] Pert, Candace B. PhD. 2006. *Everything You Need To Know To Feel Good* pp12-13 London, UK: Hay House

[56] Technically this happens through a Fourier transformation that converts a space-time co-ordinate system into a spectral co-ordinate system.

pieces, each tiny piece contains the whole picture but from a different viewpoint. Similarly, in Pribram's model of memory storage, every piece of a long-term memory is distributed over the entire dendritic arbour in a neural hologram wherein each part of the network contains information about the whole event.

Later Pribram went further to question whether the holographic wave-patterns are stored inside the brain at all? He concluded that the brain is a receiver and interpreter of waveforms rather than a storage system. In collaboration with Bohm (hence they used Bohm's quantum physics language[57] which I described in some detail in *Corporate Bitch to Shaman*) he described the brain as picking up waveforms from the 'implicate order', rendering them 'explicate'. The inforealm or field of consciousness is the implicate order whilst the physiological brain is the three dimensional explicate.

Another collaboration across disciplines has been taking place since the early 1990s, when quantum physicist Sir Roger Penrose teamed up with anaesthetist, Dr. Stuart Hameroff, to investigate consciousness. Joining together the languages of neuroscience and quantum physics, they developed a hypothesis about the actual mechanism of transfer between the brain as a storage system and the non-local, omniscient and omnipresent inforealm/holonomic brain.

The first step in this hypothesis is that it's resonant microtubules within the brain that are the physical body's link with an external consciousness. These microtubules provide the mechanism by which the holographic storage is downloaded. Hameroff gives his latest thinking in great detail in a website paper, *Quantum computation in Brain microtubules? The Penrose-Hameroff 'Orch OR' model of consciousness*[58] where 'Orch OR' stands for orchestrated objective reduction, requiring quantum coherent states and quantum computation

---

[57] Bohm, David. 1980. *'Wholeness and the Implicate Order'* U.K: Routledge & Kegan Paul

[58] http://www.quantumconsciousness.org/personal.html

at the neuronal level.

What are these microtubules within the brain and how might they link the body and the inforealm? Each brain cell has a skeletal structure and the shape of the cell is partially determined by a system of rigid but hollow, cylindrical protein beams which connect to each other with protein links and gap junctions. These are the microtubules that form the microtrabecular network. Each of these hollow, cylindrical microtubules has walls constructed of hexagonal lattices of subunit proteins known as tubulin.

Astonishingly, there are approximately 10 to the power 18 microtubules within the human brain and each of these is just five to six nanometers in diameter. This means that the giant in number microtrabecular network is functioning at close to the supersmall quantum scale in size.

Neuroscientists traditionally considered microtubules to be purely structural components of the brain but recent evidence has demonstrated that they are capable of extraordinarily fast mechanical signalling and communication functions. Each of these extraordinarily numerous and incomprehensibly tiny tubulins within the brain seems to switch on and off in the nanosecond scale. Each cell contains approximately 10 to the power 7 tubulins, and nanosecond switching predicts roughly 10 to the power 16 operations per second, per neuron. What does this superfast switching on and off mean? It creates a pulsing, electromagnetic wave that travels out from each neuron of the brain.

Recent research has also confirmed that microtubules are transient and are frequently rebuilt, in some cells several times an hour, raising a huge question around how they could possibly store information when they are in such constant flux.

It is far more plausible that they are just the resonators, the wave generators and receivers, not the storage system.

In the online paper mentioned above, Hameroff uses highly technical language that most non-specialists will not understand. But he is giving a very specific description of how these incredibly tiny microtubules, which are switching on and off at fantastically high speed, are sending out and receiving coherent waves which link from the supersmall quantum scale inside the brain to the surrounding inforealm.

He writes, *'In a panpsychist view consistent with modern physics, Planck scale*[59] *spin networks encode proto-conscious experience as well as Platonic values. Particular configurations of quantum spin geometry convey particular varieties of proto-conscious experience, meaning and aesthetics. The proposed Orch OR events occur in the brain, extending downward to processes in an experiential Planck scale medium. The basic idea is that consciousness involves brain activities coupled to self-organizing ripples in fundamental reality.*

'How can near-infinitesimal proto-conscious information link to macroscopic biology? … the Orch OR process may be an emergent phenomenon in quantum geometry mediated through London forces in hydrophobic pockets of tubulin and other proteins…

'In Orch OR pre-conscious processing is equivalent to the quantum superposition phase of quantum computation. Potential possibilities interact and then abruptly self-collapse, a slight quake in spacetime geometry. As quantum state reductions are irreversible, cascades of Orch OR events present a forward flow of subjective time and 'stream of consciousnes'' [60]

Once more everything is a probability wave of potentiality, pulsing at various frequencies, until we interact with it and force the probability wave to collapse into an observable event. To connect with Era III, the non-local mind, the world of the inforealm, the world of the shamans, we simply need to be sensitive and open enough to receive and acknowledge the waves and the impulses that we are constantly capable of accessing if we so choose.

The acknowledgement that we are receivers, downloading information from a universal consciousness, the inforealm, immediately allows the possibility of the mind changing much more quickly and radically than modern Era II neurological and psychotherapeutic theories allow. Our neural networks and the limbic attractors are capable of

---

[59] The Planck length is $1.61619926 \times 10^{-35}$ metres

[60] http://www.quantumconsciousness.org/personal.html

tapping into a much wider perception of the world and knowledge base than that which comes solely from a person's own individual life experience, or indeed that of his therapist.

And if we are receivers, we are of course also constant transmitters of information from the brain to the inforealm. Once we start to acknowledge that, then we need to be much more careful about what we say and think as both have consequences permanently stored in the universal consciousness.

Another part of the body that for many centuries has been associated with transpersonal and mythical experiences, which can be re-labelled in the language I am using here as communication with the inforealm, is the seventh chakra[61], located at the crown of the head. This seventh chakra is associated with the pineal gland, the master gland of the endocrine system. It produces the so-called spirit molecule, the hallucinogen dimethyltryptamine (DMT), a beta-carboline synthesised from melatonin, as well as at least two other hallucinogenic beta-carbolines. It has been discovered that DMT is produced endogenously within the pineal gland during birth, during death and near-death and by extremely experienced meditators during their meditation practice.

DMT is also the hallucinogenic substance contained in the chacruna leaves which are used with the monoamine oxidase inhibitor banisteriopsis caapi in the brew known as ayahuasca that Amazonian shamans drink. They claim this brew allows them to communicate directly with the plant, animal and spirit worlds, giving them the answers to any questions they choose to ask.

Thus, for centuries DMT has been produced endogenously through meditation in India and Tibet, whilst it has been taken exogenously by the shamans in Brazil and Peru. All these different people have known that somehow

---

[61] For millennia yoga and energy medicine has worked with particular energy centres called chakras. There are seven chakras located within the body, plus one below the feet and one above the crown.

the presence of DMT enhances their ability to resonate with, communicate with and receive information from the inforealm.

Whilst we can enhance this receptivity exogenously through hallucinogenics and sound such as gonging or hemi-sync[62] or chanting, the aim of Era III healing is to be able to enter this state of receptivity endogenously, through a conscious adjustment of our brain-waves.

Despite the considerable, widespread acknowledgement of DMT's potential, since 1971 Western governments have placed it on the controlled substances list, meaning that documented scientific studies on its effects are rare. I believe it is a modern tragedy that despite the vast spending on pharmaceutical pain-killers and other drugs, there is very little research being carried out into how to encourage the natural, endogenous secretion of chemicals which could lead to a vast improvement in our lives (including opiates as well as DMT). It is very easy to jump to the cynical conclusion that these chemicals are not being investigated because they would be free for everyone to use. We produce them in our own bodies and minds. They could benefit each and every one of us, but they would not benefit the medical establishment or the pharmaceutical companies.

One bright spot is that meditation is now being encouraged by many doctors, which is a great step in the right direction. But frequently it is recommended without explaining to patients how they are impacting their own physiology through their thoughts and through the meditation process and without explaining the extent to which we have choice about how to address potentially

---

[62] Hemi-sync sound is a product invented by Robert Monroe and patented by The Monroe Institute http://www.monroeinstitute.org/. It works by putting sounds of slightly different frequencies, known as binaural-beats, into the left and right ears. The brain then attempts to make a coherent whole from these vibrations, which results in the left and right hand side of the brain working together in unison, unlike normal activities which are conducted by one side or the other.

stressful situations that arise in our lives.

Summary

To summarise the material of the last three Chapters, it is our intentions, our expectations, our conditioned beliefs and our attitude of open or closed-mindedness that determine our experience, our personal 'reality'. Do we get stuck in old belief patterns or do we take responsibility to learn, evolve and grow?

The potential to download any of the information stored in the non-local inforealm via the holonomic brain connects with the ancient shamanic belief that we don't need to 'fix things' at the physical level, only at the energetic level, before they are born into physical existence. As one of my shamanic teachers said to me in a private session, *'We don't want to collapse the wave. We want to keep the potential of the whole wave as long as possible. Stay with not knowing, keep open all the possibilities.'*

All the possibilities are out there in the inforealm. We can choose to download and collapse from a probability into an event the one that serves us best. And we can ask for guidance and advice from that all-knowing source. All possibility is there, all knowledge is there. Ask and we shall receive.

Part 2: Art

Chapter 6: Era II Practices of Reconnecting Minds and Bodies and Allowing the Body to Speak

'There is no such thing as the brain, only the brain according to the right hemisphere and the brain according to the left hemisphere: the two hemispheres that bring everything into being also, inevitably, bring themselves.'[63] (Iain McGilchrist)

It has been known for many years that physiologically the left side of the brain controls the right side of the body and the right side of the brain controls the left side of the body, with the nerves crossing over in the medulla oblongata. Beyond that, there is a dawning recognition from neurological research that the two sides of the brain appear to have quite different functionality. McGilchrist's highly acclaimed work, *The Master and his Emissary* describes both the physiological and the functional differences in great detail.

In brief, some of the key physiological differences that have emerged from brain research are:

- The right hemisphere is longer, wider and generally larger as well as heavier than the left.
- There is greater dendritic overlap in the right hemisphere, that is a greater connectivity.
- There is more white matter in the right hemisphere, facilitating transfer across regions and attention to the

---

[63] McGilchrist, Iain. 2009. *The Master and his Emissary: The Divided Brain and the Making of the Western World* p.175 New Haven and London: Yale University Press

global picture.
- The hemispheres differ in their sensitivity to hormones and to pharmacological agents.
- The two hemispheres depend on different neurotransmitters (the left is more reliant on dopamine and the right is more reliant on noradrenaline).

In terms of functionality McGilchrist quotes from dozens of different studies, which together find that there is left brain dominance for local, narrowly focused attention and right brain dominance for broad, global and flexible attention. Only the right hemisphere attends to the peripheral field of vision and the learning of new information or skills. However once the skills have become familiar they shift to being the concern of the left hemisphere, which is more efficient in routine situations where things are predictable, but less efficient when assumptions have to be revised.

The outcome is that the left brain appears to operate as a very accurate but closed system. As McGilchrist describes, *'It has the advantage of perfection, but such perfection is bought ultimately at the price of emptiness, of self-reference. It can mediate knowledge only in terms of a mechanical rearrangement of other things already known. It can never really 'break out' to know anything new, because its knowledge is of its own representations only. Where the thing itself is 'present' to the right hemisphere, it is only 're-presented' by the left hemisphere, now become an* ***idea*** *of a thing. Where the right hemisphere is conscious of the Other, whatever it may be, the left hemisphere's consciousness is of itself.'*[64]

[64] McGilchrist, Iain. 2009. *The Master and his Emissary: The Divided Brain and the Making of the Western World* pp174-175 New Haven and London: Yale University Press

Functionality of the Left and Right Hemispheres of the Brain

Left Hemisphere	Right Hemisphere
Abstract and impersonal	Sees things in context
Excels at linear, sequential reasoning and systematic thought	Interested in the personal and in others as individuals
Precise and focused	Centre of empathy
The centre of language and symbol manipulation	Orbitofrontal cortex is essential to emotional understanding and regulation
Appears to see the body as an assemblage of parts, something from which we are relatively detached	Regulates the neuroendocrine interface between the body and emotions
Needs certainty, needs to be correct	Responsible for our sense of our body as something we live in
Things are explicit, compartmentalised, fragmented and static	Specialises in non-verbal communication

Later in the book he speculates that, *'It would appear that there is a good chance that the right hemisphere may be seeing more of the whole picture. Despite the left hemisphere's conviction of its own self-sufficiency, everything about the relationship of the hemispheres to one another and to reality suggests the primacy of the right hemisphere, both in grounding experience (at the bottom level) and in reconstituting left-hemisphere-processed experience once again as living (at the top level)... The value of the left hemisphere is precisely in making explicit, but this is a staging post, an intermediate level of the 'processing' of experience, never the starting point or end point, never the deepest, or the final, level. The relationship between the hemispheres is therefore highly significant for the type of world we find ourselves living in.'*[65]

He continues, *'the left hemisphere does not itself have life, such life as it appears to have coming from reconnecting with the body, emotion and experience through the right hemisphere.'* [66]

He concludes that for the good health of ourselves and of the societies that we live in, it is essential that the right brain should prevail. But unfortunately this does not seem to be where humanity is headed, for a number of reasons, two of which he describes as the asymmetry of means and the asymmetry of structure.

The asymmetry of means is the dominance of the left brain with respect to the verbal vocabulary that we all use to communicate our thoughts, feelings and concepts. *'The means of argument – the three Ls, language, logic and linearity – are all ultimately under left-hemisphere control, so that the cards are heavily stacked in favour of our conscious discourse enforcing the world view re-presented in the hemisphere which speaks, the left hemisphere, rather than the world that is present to the right hemisphere. Its point of view is always easily defensible, because analytic; the difficult lies with those who are aware that this does not exhaust the possibilities, and have nonetheless to use analytic methods to transcend analysis. It is also most easily expressible, because of language's lying in the left hemisphere: it has a voice…*

'it is hard for the right hemisphere to be heard at all: what it knows is too complex, hasn't the advantage of having been carved up into pieces that can be neatly strung together, and it hasn't got a voice anyway.'[67]

The asymmetry of structure results from the left brain being a closed system, which loops around within itself. *'The*

---

[65] McGilchrist, Iain. 2009. *The Master and his Emissary: The Divided Brain and the Making of the Western World* p.209 New Haven and London: Yale University Press

[66] McGilchrist, Iain. 2009. *The Master and his Emissary: The Divided Brain and the Making of the Western World* p.227 New Haven and London: Yale University Press

[67] McGilchrist, Iain. 2009. *The Master and his Emissary: The Divided Brain and the Making of the Western World* pp228-229 New Haven and London: Yale University Press

existence of a system of thought dependent on language automatically devalues whatever cannot be expressed in language; the process of reasoning discounts whatever cannot be reached by reasoning. In everyday life we may be willing to accept the existence of a reality beyond language or rationality, but we do so because our mind as a whole can intuit that aspects of our experience lie beyond either of these closed systems. But ***in its own terms*** *there is no way that language can break out of the world language creates... just as* ***in its own terms*** *rationality cannot break out of rationality, to an awareness of the necessity of something else, something other than itself, to underwrite its existence.*'[68]

I think we can all recognise that in modern society power, control, war and wealth are associated with the left brain way of thinking. That has led to a widespread (but thankfully not as yet completely ubiquitous) conditioning that the qualities of the left hemisphere are more valuable than the qualities of the right. We are often taught that reason is better than emotion. That science is more valuable than art. That what we see (or more accurately what we think we see) is more valuable than what we feel. That we can only trust what is physical, not what comes to us as intuition.

The result is that many of us are living primarily in our heads, not our bodies, in our logical deductions, not our experiences, in our 'shoulds' not our 'desires'.

I have many clients that initially have real difficulty in connecting with any feeling in their body. One even told me at the end of the first session that she had always thought of her body as just something to carry her head around! She had never listened to what her body was trying to tell her and the pain it was carrying.

Unfortunately, because our society has focused very strongly on what we think rather than how we feel, this is not an uncommon perception of values. But it's a misconception, a poor conditioning, as we are starting to recognise to our cost

---

[68] McGilchrist, Iain. 2009. *The Master and his Emissary: The Divided Brain and the Making of the Western World* p.229 New Haven and London: Yale University Press

and as McGilchrist highlights in his gloomy conclusion. *'So if I am right, that the story of the Western world is one of increasing left-hemisphere domination, we could not expect insight to be the keynote. Instead we would expect a sort of insouciant optimism, the sleepwalker whistling a happy tune as he ambles toward the abyss.'*[69]

'It is as though, blindly, the left hemisphere pushes on, always along the same track. Evidence of failure does not mean that we are going in the wrong direction, only that we have not gone far enough in the direction we are already headed.'[70]

I consider that part of my Era II work is to reconnect people with their right brain, bringing them back to body based experience, allowing the body to be felt, acknowledged, listened to and heard. And when I am working with people, my direct connection with their body, focusing their attention on certain areas with my hands, can speed up that process. Once more it is essential to create a safe and sacred space for allowing feelings to emerge, along with all the emotions and memories that may then surface from the body.

Integrating the hemispheres through talking to the body parts

The science of psychoneuroimmunology has demonstrated that emotions, traumas, disease, indeed the history of the individual's life in this body, are stored not only in the brain, but also in the tissues of the whole body. Every cell has memory. Every cell operates the way it does because of the ligands attached to it. And which ligands are attached to each cell depends on our endocrine system, the emotional states or moods that we have experienced in our lives.

One of the key ways that we can reconnect with our bodies is by talking to specific body parts, giving them a voice

---

[69] McGilchrist, Iain. 2009. *The Master and his Emissary: The Divided Brain and the Making of the Western World* p.237 New Haven and London: Yale University Press

[70] McGilchrist, Iain. 2009. *The Master and his Emissary: The Divided Brain and the Making of the Western World* p.235 New Haven and London: Yale University Press

of their own, allowing them to express themselves and their memories, their feelings, their needs, separate from the requirements of the loquacious left brain driven head.

With clients this approach often suggests itself to me quite quickly as I tune into the system because as I hold them I feel a strong imbalance between the left and right hand sides of the head or the left and right hand sides of the body.

I have noted the different functions of the two brain hemispheres already. This functional split has often led to the left brain (and the right side of the body) being attributed to the masculine, and the right brain (and the left side of the body) being attributed to the feminine. That is because the archetypes of the masculine are mainly seen to be physical, rational, scientific and selfish whereas the archetypes of the feminine are mainly seen to be emotional, intuitive, creative and empathic.

Ideally however, both men and women should be able to use both sides of the brain in harmony. We all have a tendency to feel more at ease in one side of the brain and the body than the other, and for some men that is in their 'feminine', for some women that is in their 'masculine', but really those labels are part of our conditioning. We all need both sets of qualities to function optimally, and as I work my intention is to help clients to bring all the parts of the system first into dialogue and then into a harmonious relationship.

But many people feel stuck in one aspect or the other, or they may intentionally be suppressing one set of qualities or the other. That usually arises from fear. It may be fear of turning into what they perceive to be the role models for either the masculine or the feminine, either because they perceive the masculine to be too angry and powerful and controlling, or because they perceive the feminine to be too weak and stupid and vulnerable. In either case it leads to an imbalanced life.

For instance, many men in the United Kingdom think it is weak to show their emotions: the 'stiff upper lip' is their conditioned state. There is no way they can ask for help, therefore they stuff their pain down and load up on stress.

Other more sensitive men express fear of stepping into their masculinity because the don't like the attributes of the male role models projected in society or they are aware of the damage that men have done to women through the ages and they don't want to repeat that pattern. They sympathise more with the qualities attributed to the feminine than the qualities attributed to the masculine.

Many women in the West think that to succeed in business they have to adopt the rational, uncaring approach, to be one of the boys. They are afraid to show their femininity because they think they will be taken advantage of and perceived as weak and vulnerable. Other women have been violated or harmed by men and are afraid of stepping into any positions of power or responsibility, taking on what they perceive to be dominating masculine attributes, therefore they choose to stay as 'weak women' rather than acting with strength and purpose.

When I am working with the body I hold it with the intention of allowing every cell and every tissue to talk and express itself if it would like to, both through voice and through movement. And as I open the space I speak aloud to the system, the body, the mind, the energy field, acknowledging that I am there to listen. That is something that the body is frequently not expecting, as very often the head attached to it consistently refuses to do just that!

It is amazing what arises when the neglected parts of the body are held and acknowledged and given permission to express themselves. Sometimes I ask the client to try to shut out the chattering head, and I may even speak to head directly, telling it that we will come back to it later and allow it to give its opinion, but first we want to listen to the other parts that wish to express themselves. Often the two legs may have very different things to say, (the left-right split) or an injured part of the body wants to be acknowledged and allowed to speak. I often invite heart to express what it would like to say, what it needs and desires if it is allowed a voice, and maybe the sexual organs.

One way of experimenting with this yourself is first of all

to put your hand on the heart centre and see if you can feel your heart beating. Don't worry if you can't! People frequently cannot initially feel their pulse at the heart centre. If that is you, then instead try to find the pulse at the neck and then follow that pulse down until you can feel the heart-beat. Sometimes this takes a while. If you are doing this yourself, be patient, allow yourself to get back into your body, acknowledging its power and its wisdom. If you are doing it with a client reassure them that they do have a heart-beat and that it may just take them some time to get in touch with it.

Even once the body parts are felt, acknowledged and allowed to speak, very often you will find that those parts don't all agree! It is very common for the head to disagree with what the heart or the sex organs or other parts of the body are expressing. These other parts may say that they want love or connection or rest, and the left brain head, the source of language and verbal communication, says that's not safe, that's not allowed. If we ask head why it is saying that, it frequently replies that it wants to protect the body and the person. This may indicate a trauma of course, with the head being associated with the left brain and the survivor part of the psyche, which wants to protect the traumatised part of the psyche whose pain is stuck within the physical body and is connected with the right brain.

Often clients find it fascinating and profound just to hear those different voices from within and to acknowledge parts of themselves which are normally not allowed to have a voice. They may see that there is an important message about how they are living their lives coming from the pain in a part of their body, if only they will listen. The danger of course is that if they don't listen, the pain will increase or spread until it reaches a level where it cannot be ignored!

Case study: Gina

Gina worked as a receptionist and only came to see me once. She told me straight away that she had abandonment issues and doesn't feel comfortable in her body. Her mother had mental health problems, was depressed throughout the pregnancy with Gina and then institutionalised when Gina was six months old.

I start feeling into the system from the root chakra. She can't get any image of little Gina. The area between the root and the heart feels very impacted. I ask her to try to breathe right down to the root whilst I use my rattle to do some cleansing of the blockage held in the energy field around the second chakra, between the root and the heart. She doesn't feel fully in her body. I ask her to hold her heart centre and I tell her that she is here, she has survived. She starts to cry – it feels very strange to hear that. She often doesn't feel she is here. What would her heart like to say if it is allowed to speak? It wants love and warmth. I ask if Gina feels she deserves that? Now she can say yes, she does! That surprises her.

Then I ask her to put her other hand on the yoni.[71] *It wants freedom. It is angry because it has been ignored for so long.*

How does head feel about all this? Terrible! The head wants to be in control. It has everything all sorted out. It is afraid of letting heart and yoni do what they want. How does that serve her? It keeps her safe.

I finish the session by asking her to look in the mirror. She finds that difficult but manages to do it, seeing that she is here and that she has choice. She acknowledges that for a bit longer she needs to be on her own, not in a relationship, because she needs to get to a place where she feels safe to be herself before she can allow someone else in. She says it feels really good for her to recognise that it is a choice to be on her own and that she can change her decision at any time.

In all cases the first step in healing is to allow the conflict between the body parts to be expressed and acknowledged. This permits the left brain and right brain ways of thinking and being, represented by the head and the body (or perhaps the survivor and the traumatised and the healthy parts), to move towards a resolution, working together rather than in conflict. When we refuse to acknowledge the body and listen to it, and instead live totally from the head, those conflicts remain suppressed and unseen, leading to disease.

Some people are initially almost totally disconnected from

---

[71] In tantric yoga all the feminine sexual organs of the first and second chakras together are known as the yoni.

their body and their feelings. Others do acknowledge that their body has painful symptoms, but they may just try to medicate away the symptoms, without investigating the cause. The danger of this approach is described brilliantly by Ruppert. *'Pain, inflammation, fever and organs that no longer function properly are our bodies' alarm signals. Our body can only express in this way that it is in danger, and that something must be done to avert the threat. These alarm signals are therefore never the real problem. As a rule they are a sensible reaction by the body to some danger. It is not a good idea to switch off any alarm without finding out what caused it to go off, and in the same way it is not advisable to remove or suppress the biological alarm signals of the body through painkillers, medication to lower the temperature, or operations on organs, without having understood why this state of alarm has arisen…*

'An acute treatment of symptoms might bring short-term relief and may even save a life but the elimination of the symptoms means that the alarm signals themselves are no longer available as an indication of the source of the danger. This means that there is a risk that illnesses can become chronic, because by suppressing the symptoms, the body will still be exposed to the damaging influences as long as they exist.'[72]

I use talking to the body parts particularly frequently with women who have suffered some form of sexual abuse, and I will talk about this further in Chapter 13, but the technique can be of use to almost anyone who wants to move towards integration and self-responsibility, growth and evolution. It helps to integrate our masculine and feminine aspects, love and consciousness, nurture and awareness, bringing these qualities into wisdom and harmony rather than conflict in our lives.

---

72 Ruppert, Franz. 2012. *Symbiosis & Autonomy, Symbiotic Trauma and Love Beyond Entanglements* pp184-185 Steyning, UK: Green Balloon Publishing

Chapter 7: Why Do We All (and Healing Practitioners More than Most) Need to Visit the Shadows?

'*Making sense of our past frees us to be present in our lives and to become the creative and active author of our own unfolding life story.*'[73](Dan Siegel)

'*Only someone who is in harmonious agreement with the past is also free for the future. One who struggles against the past remains bound to it.*'[74](Stephan Hausner)

In Chapter 3 I introduced the concept of trauma and the need to work with it in at least an Era II way, involving body and mind. Inevitably, much of the work of any practitioner concerns the difficult stuff in people's lives. Those who feel fulfilled, happy, saying yes to life, living authentically and knowing their purpose, don't usually feel they need to ask for help. Although of course, one can always be a better version of oneself. Potentially the work is never complete. There is always scope to evolve.

However practitioners are frequently helping clients to focus a light into the traumas and the repressed shadows, the stuff we don't like looking at because it makes us feel sad, angry, ashamed, guilty, etc, etc. 'Shit happens'. That's an inevitable part of the human condition, but we don't need to

---

[73] Siegel, Daniel J. 2010. *The Mindful Therapist, A Clinician's Guide to Mindsight and Neural Integration* p.70 New York, USA: W.W. Norton & Company, Inc.

[74] Hausner, Stephan. 2011. *Even if it costs me my life: Systemic Constellations and Serious Illness* p.64 Santa Cruz, CA, USA: Gestalt Press, Taylor & Francis

live in the mess or carry it around with us, allowing it to weigh us down, restrict and limit us for the rest of our lives.

As illustrated in the quotations at the beginning of this Chapter, it is increasingly being recognised that to stop the events and trauma of our past from weighing us down, eating away in our unconscious mind and impacting the health of the cells of our physical body, first we do need at least to acknowledge those painful events. That may be done through talking therapy or through physical body-mind therapy. It can be done by yourself or with a therapist/teacher. However it's approached, the intention is never to re-traumatise. The intention is to allow us to acknowledge the trauma, thereby allowing integration or release and healing to take place in a safe space. I return here to the definition of a temenos: a **protected physical** and **emotional space** in which the **transforming work of healing** takes place through **learning** and **teaching**.

Although the situation is starting to improve, the need to go to the source of the problem, sometimes known as the core wound in psychotherapy, is still not widely enough acknowledged within allopathic medicine. Too often doctors still focus on curing symptoms rather than healing causes or addressing the limiting belief system that underpins the client's disease.

An obvious example is depression. Clients frequently turn up in my therapy room with depression. Often they have been to see their family doctor, who has handed out anti-depressants without also enquiring about why the individual is depressed or giving them appropriate therapy to deal with that underlying cause. Medication may help people out of an immediate crisis or at least help them to get out of bed, and hence it may be an enabler for integrated therapy, but it can lead to a grey life of flat-lined addiction if it's not accompanied by finding out why people are depressed and then finding a suitable therapy to help them to deal with that cause.

Similarly many patients are given drugs or surgery to deal with symptoms such as heart attacks or diabetes or even cancer, without addressing the bad diet, addictions, lack of exercise or stress that have been the obvious physiological causes of the need for the medical attention and intervention. Dealing with these latter emotional causes of the physical symptoms is a clear Era II body-mind requirement, without even considering the Era III emotional or ancestral causes that may be impacting our bodies through our holominds resonating with all that is held in the holofield. As long as the symptoms are dealt with, the allopathic Era I medical system considers the patient to be cured.

I truly believe one of the gifts and advantages of integrated therapy is to get to the sources, the causes of disease and illness. As Villoldo says when he is teaching, *'If you get bitten by a snake, go to hospital immediately to get the venom removed. Then go to the shaman to ask why the snake bit you.'*

Even people who are not suffering from trauma will almost certainly have experienced difficulties and setbacks in their lives, that's why they're seeking help. Once again it returns to the fact that to resolve our pain, suffering, or discontent, that is our disease, we need to identify and acknowledge its source.

The aim of the so-called shadow work is to acknowledge our wounds and unconscious mistakes, facing the anger, guilt, shame, fear, grief and other repressed emotions that are often associated with them. Some of the experiences that we have as we do this work may initially be frightening, as they involve either a loss of control by the rational mind (and even the body) or a descent into difficult, repressed areas deep within the unconscious mind. Why would we open these new doors, not knowing what is behind them, when it might seem safer and easier to leave them locked shut?

Only by having the courage to take these traumas, wounds and 'heavy energies' (called hoocha in the shamanic world) out of the shadows, can we acknowledge them and let them go, thus healing the wounds they have inflicted on us. As we acknowledge our wounds we can ask if they also carried any gifts or lessons and then re-integrate these, whilst releasing the damage and limiting beliefs that have resulted from the shit that has happened, whatever is appropriate. In fact it is when we can look at the wounds and mistakes with compassion and without fear that we often get our greatest insights and realisations. What is key however is that this work should be done in a safe environment, a temenos space.

What is emerging in Era III (non-local through space or time) healing is that working to heal our own wounds may also involve interacting with and potentially healing both our karmic and geneological lineages. I will return to this in more detail later, but what we are carrying in our lives now may not just be from this lifetime, and in fact it may not truly be ours at all: it may belong to our ancestors or be held over in the energy field from a previous life. Working with this knowledge, outside conventional time, is a big task, but many of us are blessed to be living today in a time and a place that offers us opportunities for this type of work that our ancestors did not have.

Transference

All therapists are interacting at a very deep and close level with their clients, whether through talking or whether through engaging deep into the body's energetic field, resonating with the waves emanating from the client and downloading information from the inforealm. That inevitably leads to the danger of transference of issues between client and therapist. This is why it is widely recognised that the more work therapists have done for themselves, the better they can step into the place of helping others with their shadow work without being triggered into their own issues by the client or without becoming entangled with the client's pain.

Once more back to the wisdom of Levine. *'In the therapy situation, the therapist must strike a balance between mirroring a client's distress enough for them to learn about the client's sensations, but not so much as to increase the client's level of fear as in contagion panic. This can only happen if the therapist has learned the ins and outs of his or her own sensations and emotions and is relatively comfortable with them. Only then can we really help clients contain their troubling sensations and emotions so that they can learn that, no matter how horrible they feel, it will not go on forever.'*[75]

Because of this possibility of transference, I find it very helpful **before** a client arrives to set the stage, organise my room as a sacred space and get in touch with how I myself am feeling in the moment. Do I have any aches and pains? Is there anything bothering me? Ideally a therapist will leave all their own issues outside the door of the therapy room, but if something must come in with them because it is so present in their lives at that moment, it is best if they are consciously aware of it, physically, mentally and emotionally. That way, when they start to work with their client, hopefully they will know what is theirs and what belongs to the other.

For me personally, when I am working, sometimes I will receive information from the inforealm which manifests as physical transference, in which case I get a physical pain that mirrors a pain of the client's. On other occasions I get a feeling of imbalance between the left and right hand sides of the client's body which often represents an imbalance in or conflict between what we label the masculine and feminine parts of the person. It may for instance indicate a wounded feminine as a result of sexual abuse, abortion, surgery or infertility. Sometimes the information comes simply as words in my mind, a knowing that the client has a damaged immune system or suffered a traumatic birth and so on.

When I am aware of transference during a session, I thank the inforealm for showing me what the client's system wanted to reveal and then I ask that it is released from the place in me that it manifested. After the session, if I am still feeling something that I don't think belongs to me, there are various cleansing techniques that can be used to help release that energy that I have become entangled with. One from the shamanic field is the ritual of picking up a stone, getting in touch with the energy that I don't feel belongs to me, blowing

---

[75] Levine, Peter A. PhD. 2010. *In An Unspoken Voice: How the Body Releases Trauma and Restores Goodness* pp46-47 Berkeley, California, USA: North Atlantic Books

it into the stone, then burying the stone in the earth, asking pachamama to take the pain. Similarly I can pick up a small stick and blow what is not mine into the wood, then burn it in the fire. I can also hug a tree or take a shower, asking for the earth or the water to cleanse me.

The effectiveness of these practices derives from the symbolism of the rituals which I explain in far more detail in Chapter 14. But in brief ritual appears to serve the purpose of linking the information received by the right brain from the metaphorical, intuitive inforealm to the left brain, which is in charge of verbalising and rationalising it and integrating the information into the practical, grounded aspects of everyday life. The particular ritual of cleansing after a client also sets a clear intention that I am taking responsibility for my own health and safety.

I have learned both from my own experiences in Peru and from seeing other therapists with significant health issues, that this cleansing of anything that we absorb from clients is vitally important. I have done work in the inforealm with shamans when I have been vomiting and screaming and they have been cleansing me, cleansing me – of hoocha that was not mine and that I had taken in from others.

I have also had body therapists as clients, including massage therapists, who have not been trained to protect themselves from hoocha or to recognise transference, and who, as a result, have taken in enormous amounts of their clients' pain and trauma, possibly over years. Over a period of time their aches and pains and emotional stress have increased until in some cases they have become unable to work. I have seen similar examples in people who work in the health sector, particularly mental health, where they have become sick through entanglement with their patients' traumas.

As with many problems, the first thing for therapists facing transference issues is to be able to observe what has happened and acknowledge it, the second is to be able to release what is not truly theirs and the third is to stop the transference from happening again through methods of protecting themselves energetically.

Overall, I cannot emphasise enough the need for all practitioners to continue with their own healing journey. That is for their own health (physical, emotional and mental) and for the benefit of each one of the clients with whom they are so energetically resonant and entangled in every session.

Chapter 8: Era II and III Practices and the Ideal Client-Practitioner Space of Intention, Attention and Empathy

'*No matter how qualified or deserving you are, you will never reach a better life until you can imagine it for yourself, and allow yourself to have it.*'[76](Richard Bach)

Many people feel they have never truly been loved, and have no reference point for self-love, but virtually every therapeutic philosophy concludes that self-love is the place we need to get to in order to first of all accept ourselves just as we are and from there really begin to step into our potential. If we are ruled by fear, guilt, shame, anger, grief or the inner critic, to name just some of the possible feelings that can keep us small, then it is difficult to accept the power of self-responsibility and then start to act from a true place of choice and manifestation.

It is unfortunately incredibly rare in our society for people to be truly accepted, seen and heard, recognised and honoured without judgement and demands. It is also incredibly rare for people to be held physically and intimately without any invasive sexual intention or agenda. Because of these sad facts, a huge amount of the Era II healing available from working with a practitioner starts from the fact that the practitioner is truly present for the other. The sensitive practitioner, whether doctor or therapist, sees the other,

---

[76] Bach, Richard. 2004. *Messiah's Handbook* Charlottesville, USA: Hampton Roads Publishing Company, Inc.

listens to the other and if doing body work holds the other's system in unconditional love. For may people this is completely new. They feel they have never been allowed to express themselves through the mind and the body without judgement or demands.

In my own practice, before any healing starts I open the space for the work to take place. If it is a shamanic session then I call on the six directions of North, South, East, West, Earth and Sky and the qualities of the archetypical animals associated with the first four of these. Alternatively I use words that I was given at the Monroe Institute,[77] words which they have developed through thousands of hours of training, out of body journeying and healing experiences.

There seem to be four key elements to these words which are important for helping us to connect with the inforealm, when we are setting up an Era III healing for ourselves or others:

- **Acknowledgement** that we are more than our physical bodies and that we are about to work with a non-material energy.
- **Asking for help** from the inforealm. Depending on your belief system, this may include asking for assistance from spirits, angels, guides or divinities – anything and anyone whose information, wisdom, knowledge and experience is greater than your own.
- **Asking for protection** from this same inforealm against any entities or energies that might make the experience less than optimal for your Higher Self.
- **Giving thanks** in advance for the healing that is about to take place.

These openings are about stepping outside our normal everyday world into the ritual of healing. They are about adjusting our mental and physical vibration, our energetic transmissions outwards and setting the intention for different waveforms and energies to be received by our minds and our bodies, with the intention always being the best possible

[77] http://www.monroeinstitute.org

outcome for ourselves or the person we are working with.

Because it is incredibly important that people feel safe when doing this difficult work, I often voice aloud at the beginning of the body work session with a client that whatever arises is OK. If they want to move in any way that is fine. They do not need to lie still. If any part of the system wants to express itself, they should allow it to do that, whether through sound or movement. We are working in a space of unconditional love, where there is no right or wrong, no good or bad, and hence no judgement. Everything that arises from the shadows, no matter how painful, fearful or difficult is most welcome, because it is here to be seen and to be acknowledged, and so to be healed.

Quite often just that statement or permission voiced into the room as I hold the body opens the floodgates for expression, whether through tears, laughter, anger or body movement.

One of the keys to allowing people to feel safe and take self-responsibility, of course, is allowing them to say 'no'. Everyone needs to feel they are in charge of their own bodies and who touches them, how and where. So particularly for people who have been physically abused in some way, it can be very important initially for therapists to keep their hands off the client during the healing. Only when people feel comfortable to have hands placed on their bodies, when they say 'yes, I allow this', should the therapist make physical contact. This is the nature of the client taking self-responsibility and acknowledging their boundaries. This form of respectful and trustworthy touch from another is often a first for many people. To feel safe with physical contact may be an incredibly emotional and powerful experience. It may even be life-changing, but it cannot be forced upon anyone, it has to come from choice and will only arrive when the system feels safe.

I am indebted to one of my teachers who gave me her wisdom that it is only when therapists work from a place of unconditional love and non-judgement that they can be truly effective. I was asking her advice about a client that I was working with at the time and that I felt unsafe with. He was a drug addict with a violent history, who would never let me touch him. He always wanted the treatment to be hands off, above his body. She immediately advised me to stop working with him because as soon as a therapist's fear or judgement enters their energy field, they are not serving themselves or their client by continuing to work with them. There may be transference of the therapist's fear to the client, increasing the possibility of them responding in a way that realises that fear. Or the client may sense the therapist's judgement, making them even more entangled in their own negative feelings. There are too many risks for both parties when the therapist steps out of love and acceptance. It is no longer appropriate to be in that client-therapist relationship.

For me one of the roots of non-judgement is my belief that all of us at different times and through our different lives are victims, perpetrators and rescuers. Very, very few of us are perfectly evolved and healed, working in the service of others lifetime after lifetime. In particular, when we recognise that we are all capable of holding all these opposing positions, it compassionately helps us to accept others who may present themselves primarily as perpetrators at this moment in time.

I remember a telephone conversation with one potential client who had been a drug addict, professional fighter and convict in the past. He assured me he was now free of dependency and violence and wanted to work with me. During our conversation he presented himself with true integrity and openness and this convinced me to see him despite some initial fear that arose in me as he started telling his story. He was an amazing person! He was currently working with kids on the street that he was totally able to relate to. Some of them were potentially violent but they respected him and knew he wouldn't take any bullshit from them. He had stepped from perpetrator and victim to rescuer, but knew he had more work to do. I felt totally safe when I was in the room with him and had huge admiration for him. But of course it would have been so easy initially to judge him in that first conversation and then refuse to work with him.

That would have been my problem, my fear and my loss, not his!

However, in the rare instances when I do come across potential clients that I don't feel I can work with without my own judgement or fear coming into the room, I don't work with them at all. That appears to be of the greatest service all round, but of course is only possible because I work in the private sector where the clients and I both have choice. Unfortunately this is not always possible in the public sector, where therapists and patients are assigned to each other by the system. And that may be one of the reasons why private treatments often get better results – the practitioners and clients have chosen to work with each other!

A really difficult area for integrated healthcare practitioners can be when there are signs or a history of mental instability or psychosis. I certainly don't have the medical training to be able to make a proper clinical diagnosis in such cases. Many of the people that come to integrated healthcare practitioners do believe they hear voices, or work with guides, or angels, or spirit animals or ancestors. Many family doctors would immediately refer such people for psychiatric assessment. By and large I want to support these people in their connections with the inforealm which is where this information may genuinely be coming from. For the most part those who receive such information are sensitive, evolved people open to the Akashic experience.

However sometimes individuals may **not** be participating in an evolved communication with the inforealm, they may be suffering from serious mental disturbances and psychosis. It is always up to the individual practitioner to decide if they can work with someone or if they feel it is best to refer them elsewhere.

Having said that, what I have experienced personally and how I work would frequently be seen by the outside world to be pure imagination at best or delusion at worst. I am walking a tightrope as I do this work. My own belief is that some of it is genuinely in the realm of Era III healing, but it's important not to forget that some of it is extremely powerful Era II healing, invoking the power of the placebo. For example, if a client believes they have an entity and they believe that I have removed it, that belief makes them feel better. Often I do genuinely believe I have done that particular piece of extraction work and I follow up with a ceremony afterwards for the entity as described later on. Sometimes I may be less certain regarding the origins of the client's sensation of a psychic attack, but to a large extent as long as the work I am doing benefits the client, to me it is irrelevant whether it is genuine Era III healing or successful through the psychosomatic effect of Era II healing.

How much of the story does the practitioner need to know?

Another frequent difference in the approaches of Era I and Era II and III healers is how much information the client needs to disclose before starting to work. In Era III healing I don't necessarily want to get too embroiled in the story, but of course as a therapist if the client comes with an issue that they specifically want me to work with, that is absolutely fine and they are always free to tell me what that is.

When new clients come to me now, particularly for Reiki or craniosacral therapy, I give them a choice. I ask them whether they would simply like to lie down and I will start to feel into the system, and as I am working I will tell them what I sense and see if it resonates with them. Alternatively, if there is something specific they want to address, then of course I will work with them on that particular issue.

It is approximately half and half between people who are happy to just see what happens and how their system presents and those who have a specific problem that has brought them to see me and which they want to describe and work with.

What I no longer do in either instance is take a detailed case history, in direct contradiction to the Western medical profession. There are a number of reasons for this.

First, if someone comes in with a detailed tale of woe, it can be confusing regarding where to start. For instance, suppose a new client arrives with the following story: 'I am

Jewish and all my ancestors were killed in the Holocaust, except my mother, who was raped and became pregnant with me, but then she died in child-birth, and I had a series of sexually and physically abusive foster parents. When I was 16 I tried to commit suicide, but I even failed at that. I moved to a new country where I managed to get a job in a restaurant, but then I had a car accident and broke my leg so I lost my job. I have had two abortions, and now I am unemployed and depressed with chronic back pain and migraines. I have been taking anti-depressants for the last five years, but they don't seem to be helping.' (This is not actually a single client's story, but I have heard each part of this story from several different people over the years in various combinations.)

At this point it is very easy to get caught up in the story. And to feel overwhelmed as a result! Where on earth to start?

What I have learned through experience is that some things may indeed have happened, but they may no longer be relevant or causing any problems. The body may have healed from some or all of these events, the client may have done a lot of personal work around these traumas or accidents, such that there may no longer be anything stuck in the physical or energetic body to deal with. However, when I get the historical list of physical, mental and emotional problems, I don't know which are still causing 'dis-ease'.

A slightly different problem is that the system may not be ready to divulge its deepest secrets immediately, particularly if the client has never done any body work or inner healing work. A detailed questioning and case history may either lead to the client lying and hiding something, or force an issue into the open too quickly, in a way that risks causing mild or severe re-traumatisation. In this regard integrated healthcare therapists often refer to working with the system as being like peeling an onion, where the layers come off gradually. On the outside may be the most accessible but also the most superficial problems. As we move in towards the centre, we approach the core wounds, the deep and chronic beliefs which keep the person stuck and in pain. If coming to see me is the first step that someone is taking on their healing journey, I would be reluctant to jump straight into shamanic work which is frequently very fast and deep, and maybe too intense for some people whose survival self has never allowed them to look at the trauma or the mistakes they have made. Craniosacral, Reiki and holistic body work in my experience tend to be more gentle and help to open up the system layer by layer, allowing the client always to feel safe during the process.

People who come to me specifically requesting shamanic healing have usually done a lot of work on themselves already and have an issue that they specifically do want to deal with. In these cases I ask them to tell me a little bit about the issue, and I may ask some questions about the family, or how long they have felt that this problem was impacting their lives, but again I try not to get too embroiled in the story. Indeed those who tell very traumatic stories fluidly and without emotion, may well be telling them from a place of deep disassociation. In these cases it is important for people to get out of the verbal head story (the left brain) into the feeling body story (the right brain) as soon as possible, because the body never lies! It just needs to be listened to, in a safe environment.

Despite what I have just said, two questions that I think are important are first, whether the person is on any medication? This will impact how the system feels and I want to be aware of it for instance when asking for toxins to be released from the system.

Some therapists, such as Ruppert, believe that if a client is on certain psychotic drugs you should not agree to work with them. He writes, '*In my opinion, it is essentially not possible to carry out cause-oriented therapy with people who are trying to keep their internal emotional chaos under control with high doses of psychotropic drugs, because the reduction in emotional affect means that the trauma events in the background cannot be reconstructed. Under medication, it is hardly feasible during therapy to achieve even part of a re-emergence of the trauma feelings in order to use this experience to arrive at their cause.'*[78]

Each therapist must make their own call on this issue and how they want to handle it, but it is important in any case to know the answer to the medication question.

The second question, for any woman of child-bearing age is are they pregnant? If they are, then the therapist is immediately dealing with two people, not just one, and the session needs to reflect that.

In some cases, depending on what emerges in the initial conversation, I may also ask a client about their spiritual belief system, if any, because I consider it to be essential to work in accordance with their belief system. For example if someone comes who is an atheist with no concept of anything beyond death, they may just want to feel better here and now, and there is absolutely no point in me explicitly doing any work that involves a soul concept, because that would be imposing my belief system on them. Shamans would say that is starting to get into the dark side, sorcery, imposing something on another energetically, without their permission.

As a healer it is very important to acknowledge that we never know what is in the best interests of a client's Higher Self. It is easy to hold an egotistical desire for clients to feel wonderful after a session and for their problems to resolve or for their physical health to improve, but that is not what it's about! Everyone dies at some point and people who seek therapy may be terminally ill. But they may still be able to resolve and heal a great number of issues before their death. There may be family entanglements and divides that can be seen and resolved, with massive healing not only to the individual but also to others in their family system. There may be guilt, shame or fear about a whole range of issues that can be cleared before death. There may be limiting beliefs about being unworthy, ugly, unlovable, that can be seen and altered.

---

[78] Ruppert, Franz. 2012. *Symbiosis & Autonomy, Symbiotic Trauma and Love Beyond Entanglements* p.183 Steyning, UK: Green Balloon Publishing

The way I approach things is always for healing causes, not curing symptoms, on the underlying assumption that our souls carry forward into the next life, and hence the more we can evolve and release karmic suffering and burdens in this life, the healthier and lighter our starting position becomes the next time around. (In a session of course I can only work with that attitude as long as it is not at odds with the client's belief system.) But I need to work from a place of trust rather than attachment to the outcome of any session.

Victim, rescuer, perpetrator triangle

This triangle of interconnectedness is discussed within much psychological and complementary therapy training and the advice is almost always for the therapist to stand outside the triangle as much as possible. Indeed we are often assisting our clients to escape from this triangle, where they may have got stuck primarily in one of the positions.

At least initially, clients who come seeking help are frequently used to seeing themselves as victims. That is the role they have adopted, consciously or unconsciously, in their family or society and hence they may want a therapist to be a rescuer. Demonstrating this, I have explicitly had clients call me up to make an appointment or even walk in to a first appointment and ask, 'So can you fix me?' The answer is no! The only person that can fix you is yourself, although a therapist may be able to guide you or suggest exercises for you to do or help you see things from a new perspective or be the channel for you to connect to your own innate self-healing wisdom and capabilities.

But as a therapist I am aware that I need to be very careful of not stepping into a rescuer role, which keeps the client as a victim and risks creating a model for co-dependence.

Ruppert explains the significant effort required from therapists who like to be rescuers. *'Recognising that one cannot help traumatised people if they do not want to address and work on their trauma themselves, or are unable to, requires a conscious decision not to empathise immediately nor to be continually concerned about the best way to help.'*[79]

In cases of trauma, therapists must be particularly careful about assuming any power, as unconsciously clients who have been traumatised may want to be victims. Their patterning as a result of their conditioning, may be to look for someone to take control, to assume power, to be the perpetrator. In these cases therapists need to be aware of the potential for the victim-perpetrator dynamic as well as the victim-rescuer dynamic and stay as clear of it as possible.

Ruppert writes, *'Many relationships would collapse like a house of cards if the person who sees himself as of no importance would realise that the simple reason the other is more powerful is because he, the submissive one, regards him as such.'*[80]

As a therapist I recognise I must always avoid stepping into a position of power! Therapists are most effective if they have humility and work from a sense of love rather than ego. This is another reason why therapists constantly need to be engaged in their own personal development and cleansing, releasing their own symbiotic entanglements and ego driven desires for success.

Working with babies and pregnant women

Often students ask me if it is OK to work with pregnant women. For me the answer is definitely yes. There is reluctance from some therapeutic organisations to make such a recommendation because as we live in an increasingly litigious society, organisations are worried that if a woman miscarries or if something is wrong with the baby, the therapist might be blamed or even sued. This is working from a place of fear and does not seem to be a helpful, compassionate, trusting attitude.

---

[79] Ruppert, Franz. 2012. *Symbiosis & Autonomy, Symbiotic Trauma and Love Beyond Entanglements* p.251 Steyning, UK: Green Balloon Publishing

[80] Ruppert, Franz. 2012. *Symbiosis & Autonomy, Symbiotic Trauma and Love Beyond Entanglements* p.56 Steyning, UK: Green Balloon Publishing

When I am working with a pregnant woman, I always acknowledge that I am working with two souls and I ask the universal energy to assist each of these souls in the best way possible, at the physical, mental and emotional levels.

Babies in the womb or children in the first few years of life are the one exception I have to the rule that I can only treat with explicit consent. I have always been taught only to give healing to those who ask for it – otherwise it is uninvited intervention in a soul's path and becomes akin to sorcery. Even when working with a fetus or a non-verbal child I am always asking for their energetic permission, but of course it is not then explicit, only felt. If for any reason I felt I didn't have the child's permission then I would not work on the first three chakras of the mother to avoid energetic entanglement with the baby in the womb.

Overall, the more we learn about the infant in the womb, the more it becomes clear that how the parents (particularly the mother) are feeling about themselves and the pregnancy, has as enormous impact on the unborn child. This means that any assistance we can give to the mother at that critical time for the child, to de-stress, to love herself, or to sort out her own symbiotic family entanglements, the better a chance that child has, right from the start of its life.

During the birth process itself many children experience severe trauma as they come down the birth canal. They are potentially being bombarded by drugs, forceps, ventouse machines, scalp monitors and so on, in addition to the normal pressures of the contractions as they are pushed out from the womb. They may be pulled out at unnatural angles or there may be caesarians where they don't experience the gradual, natural pushing, but instead are instantaneously transported from the liquid, enclosed womb, with all its support and noise and warmth and darkness, to the bright, harsh isolation of the operating room.

In some cases babies may be taken away immediately after birth and prior to any contact with the mother to an incubator or emergency treatment room. This is all done with the best of intentions by the medical team, it's done out of love and a desire for their child to survive by the parents, but it can set the foundation for shock and abandonment. I have worked with a number of clients that were premature. With their logical minds they know they were wanted. They know they were always loved. But as tiny babies they didn't get physical contact. They were isolated and at their core they feel abandoned and unloved.

Babies suffering from birth trauma usually respond very quickly to treatment. Yes, the past lives may still be there in the Akashic energy field, but in the current body the trauma is very recent and quite specific. It has not yet been stuck in the system for decades, there are no entrenched limbic attractors. In these cases information that allows change in the system usually comes through very quickly, as babies are usually very open and non-resistant to change. They are not yet conditioned to a particular limiting belief by the society around them.

Mothers too often have a traumatic time during the birth process and some of the women I have worked with have beaten themselves up a lot afterwards because they wanted natural births, they had been to all the classes, they had written a birthing plan. Then it didn't go according to plan and they ended up with drugs, epidurals and potentially caesarians. In addition to their physical pain they may feel guilt and failure. That can knock on. Sometimes they experience problems with breast-feeding. Sometimes they suffer from depression. They can easily get into a vicious cycle of a sense of failure, depression, abandonment of care for the baby, even more failure…

These mothers need to seek help as soon as possible. There may be genuine physical problems, which for instance may need a pelvic alignment using craniosacral therapy, or a Reiki treatment might help them to release the residual pharmacological drugs stuck in the system. Alternatively or additionally, body work can help them to acknowledge and then release emotional problems arising from the birth, assisting them to look to the future rather than getting stuck in the trauma and pain of the birth and its immediate aftermath.

The bottom line is that it is advantageous for the whole system, infants, mothers and the rest of the family, to get help as soon as possible!

In my training course at the College of Craniosacral Therapy, Thomas Atlee told an archetypal story of the child who is born by emergency caesarian after a difficult and non-successful passage through the birth canal. As I recall it goes something like this. After the birth the child is stressed and as a result the pyloric valve has a tendency to stay shut in the fight or flight position, rather than the open feeding and digestive position. The baby cries a lot because it is hungry, but then it cannot digest its food properly and cries because it is in pain. It regurgitates milk and constantly wants to feed but doesn't keep anything down. The parents get increasingly anxious and over time perhaps angry. The baby is always sick and irritated. The parents' stress levels rise, they start shouting at each other and at the baby. They can't sleep because the baby is always crying, as a result of which their stress levels rise even further and their immune systems are weakened, making them prone to viruses and infections. The household has the potential to turn into a nightmare for everyone, dominated by stress, anger, violence and a hatred for the baby. The vicious cycle is set in place for the baby to feel unloved and unwanted, to be abused physically and emotionally and to turn into an unhappy, stressed, depressed child who may withdraw at school because they doesn't know how to react to people, or who may in turn become a bully, because that is the only parental role model they know.

If the same baby is given appropriate early treatment to release the birth trauma, then the pyloric valve can open correctly when the child is feeding, it doesn't get sick after feeding, it only cries when it is hungry, until food is offered and absorbed. It smiles at its parents, who smile back and tell it what a wonderful, sweet child it is. They bond as a family unit and the child sleeps for most of the night, allowing the parents to rest too. The virtuous cycle is set in place for the baby to feel nourished and loved, whilst the parents are proud and nurturing of each other and the child.

The whole family's prospects look completely different and all because the child was given early treatment to release the shock of a difficult birth.

What will happen in a healing session and afterwards?

Clients often ask me that question and the answer is, 'I don't know'!

Once someone lies down on the table and I tune into their system, I just trust that it will reveal what it wants to show me today, at this time. I allow it to give me information and allow knowledge and healing to flow through me (as a conduit) from the inforealm. I try to accept whatever I am experiencing, allowing information to download from the external consciousness and helping the client to open themselves to resonance with the holographic universe. I just need to feel into what is happening, to experience it, I don't need to make sense of it, I don't need to understand the information. Whenever I am not sure, I ask for guidance and then stand back without trying to probe too hard.

I ask my clients to try to stay awake and to be aware of what they are sensing as they lie on the table, but sometimes, if people are exhausted and stressed, as they relax they go to sleep. That's fine, the work will still be taking place in the system, but I prefer it if people can stay conscious and aware of the feelings in their body.

Frequently as clients enter an Era III healing situation they may feel as if there is more than one pair of hands working on them, more 'people' in the room than are physically present. Also they may feel as if a therapist's hands are one part of the body when actually they are on another. This is nothing to worry about, it may be the energy field connecting with the inforealm or the interconnectedness of the physical body allowing the source of the pain and the referral place of its manifestation to communicate and be acknowledged.

Clients also quite frequently report intense sensations in

parts of their body, such as feeling icy cold, or as if they are on fire. This may arise because the energy floods in or out of a certain area, or it may arise because a memory is triggered from the unconscious mind which could involve extreme heat or cold.

Visions are also common with body Era II and Era III body work, including colours and tunnels spiralling either vertically or horizontally with lights, people, religious figures or animals at the end of them.

Memories of things that happened years ago and that the client hasn't thought about for a long, long time may emerge.

People from the past may come to mind, including those that have died. In this case I encourage the client to ask if there is a message from these people, something they want the client to know, some gift they wish them to have.

Visions of events that the client doesn't recognise at all may arise, in which case they may be entering a past life scenario.

In all cases I ask the client to try to allow whatever comes, observing it without fear, maybe dialoguing if they meet with someone, but without trying to understand the story from the rational, conscious mind. Just allow the experience and the information received.

Another sensation I personally have experienced quite often, particularly when I was working at The Monroe Institute and in ayahuasca ceremonies, is a sense of being examined. It feels as if little bugs or figures are crawling over me, working on me. I have also had a sense on a number of occasions of being in a laboratory or hospital with people working on me with instruments and making adjustments somewhere in my system or energy field.

And sometimes it is huge emotions that come. Fear, pain, shame, guilt, sadness, grief, anger. They are all welcome. They are all there to be seen, to be acknowledged and to be integrated or released, whatever is best for our healing at that moment in time, in the temenos space.

Because every one of these sessions is different, after a session the client may feel totally elated: light and energised and ready to dance in joy. Or they may feel drained, physically exhausted, ready to sleep for two days. Everyone's life experience is different, therefore what happens in the healing space is different. What I do know is that these experiences, although quite brief, are frequently life changing.

The beautiful thing is that when we work deep in the energy field in this way, things can happen really quickly. The intention is always to connect with the inforealm, the source of all knowledge, to allow us to acknowledge that we have choice, to see that the future can be different from the past, to release our limiting beliefs and our stuck patterns. The intention is to give us the wisdom and knowledge needed to step into our potential, our magnificence, creating our own destiny. This is where the shamanic approach and body work do clearly split from at least some forms of psychotherapy.

Chapter 9: Reiki: one of the most readily available forms of Era III healing

'*Reiki is love, and in this time of planetary crisis, we all need all the love we can get.*'[81] (Diane Stein)

Reiki, literally translated, means the Universal Energy, hence its intention right from the start is to be an Era III healing, even when the therapist is in the same room as the client.

Within the Reiki tradition there are three levels of 'attunement' to this energy. Level 1 allows self-healing, Level 2 allows people to work with others and Level 3 allows people to teach others. Traditionally Level 3 was only passed on to people who had been working at the Level 2 stage for many years and had gained significant experience, before stepping into the role of teacher or Master. Unfortunately that is no longer always the case, which is why Reiki's reputation has to some extent been undermined in the UK at least.

Reiki has always started with self-healing. This was clearly a sensible strategy from its inception, since, as I have mentioned frequently already, it's increasingly widely recognised that the more healed the therapist, the more present and loving they can be with another, without getting caught up in fear and judgement and transference. The first step on any healing journey is working with ourselves.

The five principles of Reiki are:

- Just for today I will give thanks for my many blessings

---

[81] Stein, Diane. 1995. *Essential Reiki: A complete guide to an ancient healing art* p.15 Freedom, CA, USA: The Crossing Press, Inc.

- Just for today I will not worry
- Just for today I will not be angry
- Just for today I will do my work honestly
- Just for today I will be kind to my neighbour and every living thing

Why are they all just for today? Historically I don't know, that's just how they are taught, but my own feeling is that it is an acknowledgement of the wisdom of living in the present. If we live focused on the past we live with our old fears, our wounds and our immature self. If we focus on the future we live a false projection. Only in the present time can we be truly alive, only now can we have new and genuine experiences and actions. Only now can we not worry, not be angry, live happily, live joyously.

In a traditional Reiki session, whether for self-healing or healing others, the practitioner works through the energy centres, traditionally known as the chakras, starting at the crown and working down through the root (perineum) before working on the legs and finishing at the feet.

The major features attributed to each chakra and their associated organs in the endocrine system and the nervous system are shown in the table below.

Chakra	Name	Colour	Element	Endocrine Gland	Nervous Plexus
First	Base or root	Red	Earth	Gonads (testes and ovaries)	Coccygeal
Second	Sacral	Orange	Water	Adrenals and gonads	Sacral
Third	Solar Plexus	Yellow	Fire	Adrenals and pancreas	Solar
Fourth	Heart	Green/Rose	Air	Thymus	Cardiac/ pulmonary
Fifth	Throat	Blue	Ether	Thyroid and para-thyroid	Laryngeal
Sixth	Third Eye	Indigo	Vibration	Pituitary	Brain
Seventh	Crown	Violet/White	Spiritual Vibration	Pineal	Brain

When a student feels they are ready to move on to healing others, usually several months after receiving Reiki 1 and having worked regularly on themselves, they receive a Reiki level 2 attunement, in which they are given three symbols to use: Cho Ku Rei, Sei Hei Ki and Hon Sha Zei Sho Nen.

Cho Ku Rei

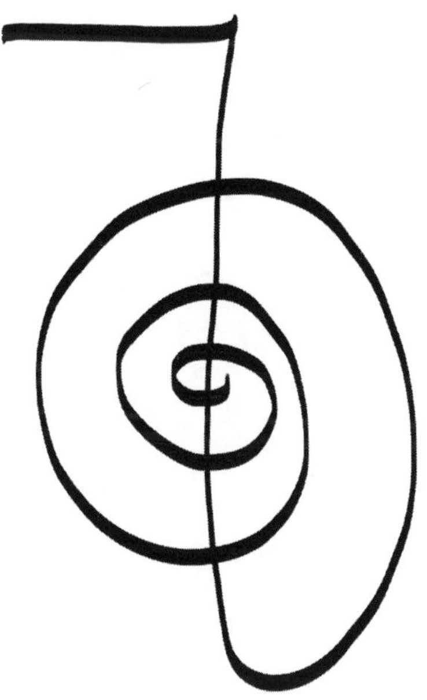

fig:6

Cho Ku Rei is the power symbol and means *put all the power of the universe here*. The straight lines represent energy and the spiral represents the physical body. Where the vertical crosses the spiral represents the chakras.

Sei Hei Ki

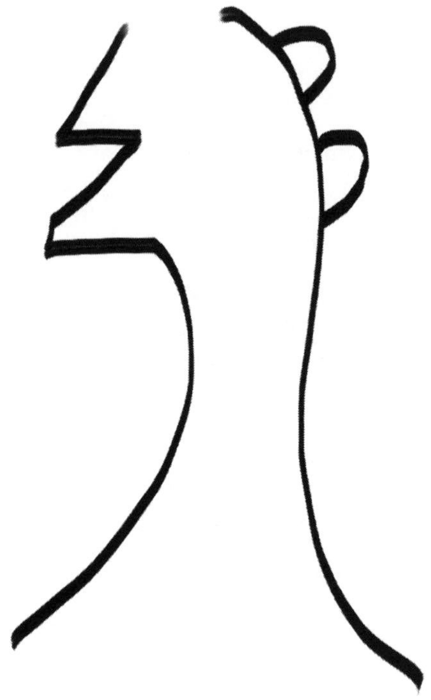

fig:7

Sei Hei Ki is the mental and emotional symbol. It means *God and humanity joined together in love, wisdom and harmony* and it helps to balance the right and left sides of the brain.

Hon Sha Zei Sho Nen

fig:8

Hon Sha Zei Sho Nen is the distance symbol and means *the God consciousness in me reaches out to the God consciousness in you, in love, wisdom and harmony*. The top six lines represent no past, seven to fifteen represent no present and sixteen to twenty-two represent no future. This symbol is appropriate because we are working outside normal space and time as we do distance healing.

When doing a Reiki session, I open the healing space as usual, (see Chapter 8) and then I specifically and very intentionally call in the Reiki energy at three levels: physical, mental and emotional. Above this I am always asking the Reiki to work for the best interests of the client's Higher Self, which I am unaware of.

I do this very intentionally because I do believe that Reiki can be harmful if it is used without clear intention and presence. I am aware that that is a highly contentious statement, but it is how I work based not only on my own experience, but the massive experience of some of my highly respected teachers.

Early in 2014 there was a question posed in a Reiki sharing group on LinkedIn regarding whether Reiki could ever do harm. There was an avalanche of responses, ranging from 'absolutely not - Reiki is pure love, Reiki is God's energy', to 'absolutely yes', for a variety of reasons. There was a reasonable consensus however that whatever we believe Reiki itself to be, the therapist is also in the room. As a result, their energy and intentions are also crucial and they are acting as a channel or transmitter, therefore they may be adding to or interfering with the energy coming through them.

To make my intentions totally clear as I am connecting with the inforealm, when I call the Reiki energy in at the physical level, I always ask that each and every physical cell should work optimally, in the perfect template of health, if that is possible. If that is not possible I ask the Reiki energy to help to release those cells that cannot work optimally from the body as toxins, in whatever way is safe, to be replaced by cells that are working beautifully and optimally, in the perfect template of health.

The reason for this is that some cells, such as cancers and tumors, appear to love energy. I prefer to be very clear that I am not just channelling energy into each and every cell. I am channelling the energy in for the optimal performance of each cell, in line with the best interest of the person's Higher Self. In practice I have found this to be extremely useful for people with scar tissue, as it appears to help to dissolve the scar tissue, which cannot necessarily be healed, but can be released from the body.

Some people may say this is semantics, but for me it is both working from a place of authenticity with my intention and it has proven effective in a number of cases with myself and clients. Like prayer, healing intention has to be semantically well designed and clear. If you pray for money a member of your family might die and leave you a fortune, so be specific!

I go on to call in the Reiki energy at the emotional level, asking the Universal Energy to help allow the emotional energy field to flow freely and without blockages. And I ask for any impact that emotional blocks are having on the physical body to be released, in the best way possible for the client's Higher Self.

Finally at the mental level I ask the Universal Energy to help allow the mental energy field to flow freely and without blockages, taking mental energy from where it is too bright or too hot to areas where it is not bright enough or too cold. And I ask for any impact that mental energy blocks are having on the physical body to be released, in the best way possible for the client's Higher Self and purpose.

In a traditional Reiki healing, the therapist starts at the client's head and then moves on down through each chakra, feeling for blockages, pain or imbalance, then moving to the knees, ankles and feet. Craniosacral therapy also tunes in to the client's system but then the therapist moves their hands and their intention to wherever they feel is necessary, rather than just working with the specific chakra centres.

Personally, even if I am doing a Reiki session, I always allow myself to be guided by where the client's system wants to be held. For instance, if there is a shoulder injury, or a wrist or hand injury, I will absolutely go to that place as well as the traditional Reiki positions. This is partly because I find it easier to sense what is going on when I feel into the place of the pain or injury, partly because the client feels better when I acknowledge and hold the place of pain or injury (this of course may be attributed to the placebo effect) and partly because I may then feel an energetic blockage that I specifically want to focus on removing. That's what works for me, but other Reiki Masters will say it doesn't matter where you hold the body, the Reiki knows where it needs to go and works accordingly.

With either Reiki or craniosacral treatments, once the system reveals a problem, I focus on whether it has a physical, mental or emotional cause. There is also the issue of the time frame associated with the problem. Is it relatively new or very ancient? Is it something that originated during the birthing process? Is it something brought in from a past life? Is it the result of a recent accident or trauma? Is it associated with pharmaceutical or recreational drugs? I simply ask the system to show me what it needs at this time and am guided by whatever answer comes to me from either the client or the inforealm, the Universal Energy.

On the subject of medications, I have quite a lot of clients that dislike and try to avoid taking pharmaceutical drugs, but sometimes it is necessary for them to do so for a variety of different reasons. What I advise is to bless these medications before taking them. Then they are being absorbed into the body with a loving intention and a request for help, not with resentment or anger. And it is important that as a therapist works they should not be encouraging these medications to leave the system, even if the system does perceive them as toxins (which is more likely if you have taken them with anger and resentment). That's one of the reasons it is important to know before a treatment if a client is on any medications. Then these medications can be requested to focus on the cells where they can best assist the client's Higher Self, with the least damage elsewhere.

The evidence I have from reading and personal experience is that in the inforealm this request and intention does make a difference. For instance the Monroe Institute sells audio CDs for cancer patients to take alongside chemotherapy or radiation treatment and these appear to allow the drugs to work with far fewer side-effects than usual elsewhere in the body.[82] Similarly, the Masaru Emoto work on crystallised water[83] demonstrates very clearly that the structure of the water molecules changes when given love and encouragement rather than hate and fear. Would you rather take a medication with the former or the latter energy bearing in mind that you are eighty per cent liquid?

There are mountains of evidence that Reiki and other energy healing does work, through both space and time. Two good sources for this evidence for those that want to see the results are the research papers on The Monroe Institute website[84]and The Soul Medicine Institute website.[85] The latter has set up the first international database of energy psychology case histories, which collects medical and psychiatric diagnoses before treatment. It notes the energy psychology treatments used and the diagnosis after treatment. It is peer reviewed and conforms to the Consort Standards and the Standards of the National Institutes of Health.

In a book based on the results reported to the Institute,[86] Dawson Church and Norman Shealy, M.D., Ph.D. document over one hundred scientific studies and dozens of medically verified 'miraculous' cures, that demonstrate the power of thought, prayer and belief. Based on their evidence, they identify the three pillars of Soul Medicine as being energy, intention and consciousness.

Once again it is the transmission and reception of waves, focusing on the outcome we desire and interacting with the infinite array of possibilities contained in the inforealm using our holonomic brains, that together produce through the collapse of the probability wave to an observable event, what might appear to Era I medical practitioners to be miracles.

---

[82] http://www.monroeinstitute.org/research/cat/cancer/taking-the-sting-out-of-cancer-treatment

[83] http://www.masaru-emoto.net/english/water-crystal.html

[84] http://www.monroeinstitute.org

[85] http://www.soulmedicineinstitute.org/home.html

[86] Shealy, M.D., Ph.D., Norman and Church Ph.D., Dawson. 2008. *Soul Medicine: Awakening your Inner Blueprint for Abundant Health and Energy* USA: Energy Psychology Press

Chapter 10: Shamanic Healing

'The great intellectual and emotional change accompanying the paradigm shift will be in people's ability to accept not having full explanations; they will understand that the depth of the mystery exceeds explanations.'[87] (Terence McKenna)

Recently I gave a talk to a group of people who knew very little about shamanism, and before I started I asked them for some of their ideas about what a shaman does. Most of them came up with a spiritual connection and an indigenous, tribal link. Some used the word primitive, and quite a few had a negative impression, perceiving shamans as dangerous and focusing on the 'black magic' aspects rather than healing.

So, since I work as a shamanic practitioner, and I am about to describe some shamanic techniques, let me give you first of all my definition of what a shaman does:

Shamans have been around for thousands of years, in most of the indigenous tribes across the world. They have been the doctors and the healers in the tribes. As well as dealing with physical illness, the distinguishing skills of a shaman have included:

- being able to work outside physical space and time;
- seeing the energy body surrounding the physical body and any blockages in it;
- working in the spirit world, with the ancestors;
- accessing the soul and its past lives as well as the physical body in the present life;
- connecting with the rocks, plants and animals and their

[87] Sheldrake, Rupert, McKenna, Terence and Abraham, Ralph. 1992. *Chaos, Creativity and Consciousness* p.62 Rochester, Vermont, USA: Park Street Press

wisdom and knowledge, honouring all life on this planet; and
- accepting that all things on this planet are interconnected and live in symbiosis.

Frequently shamans go on what they describe as 'a journey', as they voyage outside their physical body, connecting with information contained in what I have been calling the inforealm. Traditionally shamans would call it connecting with Spirit. The success of shamanic healings and guidance in diverse tribes around the world, over centuries, is one of the clearest demonstrations that Era III healings are effective.

London is a very multi-cultural city and my clients come from all parts of the planet. I attract many people from cultures and countries that believe in shamanism, such as South America and Africa, as well as from cultures that believe in re-incarnation, such as India and China. But I also attract a high proportion of immigrants who have no shamanic or karmic beliefs, including those from white European backgrounds. These people often carry the particular traumas of displacement and of not living in the land of their culture and their ancestors: very traditional shamanic issues!

Within the immigrant group from traditionally shamanic cultures, my clients do fairly frequently come with a sense of being under ritualistic attack. Don Heberto, one of my Shipibo teachers in the Amazon, is keen to make the distinction within shamans between the curanderos: the shamans who work for healing, and the brujas: the sorcerers who interfere in everything from girls asking that a particular man will marry them to sending sickness to a rival or enemy.

There is a knife-edge in shamanism between service and sorcery. This is acknowledged in shamanistic societies, but the possibility of doing harm through our thoughts or our wishes is less accepted in Western societies. If you believe that is possible, then most of us will most likely have stepped into sorcery at some point, perhaps without real intention, from the unconscious mind. But unfortunately in a number of cultures around the world this sorcery is still entirely intentional and malevolently directed.

I have been taught that, without any intention of malevolence, and indeed even with an intention to be of service, as soon as we decide there is something 'wrong' with someone and we try to 'fix' them, if we don't have their permission to work with them, we are engaging in sorcery. I am aware that this is a contentious statement. Many Reiki healers believe it is fine to send distance healing to people that have not requested it (perhaps because the family or friends of the sick person want to send them healing and have requested it, without asking permission from the sick person). Many Buddhists send healing thoughts to people that have antagonised them in some way, and to people they don't even know, in a practice known as Loving Kindness or Metta Bhavana. The intention of this practice is undoubtedly benevolent, but it is being done without the permission of the recipient.

More obviously, as soon as we talk about someone behind his or her back, wishing them ill or judging them, we are engaging in sorcery. If you listen to gossip you are just as guilty as the person who is doing the gossiping for you are fuelling those negative statements and intentions. Be careful what you say, be careful what you wish for. You may not think you are doing any harm but as soon as you recognise the ripples every thought and every action has in the inforealm, you are capable of interfering with others, hurting them through what are known as psychic daggers or black magic.

So is there a potential downside of shamanism? Undoubtedly yes. But if a shaman is practising sorcery it is being done consciously, with the intention of harming the target, whereas there is a similar potential harm to others from every malicious thought we have and every ill-wishing, judgemental statement we make, although these may be less conscious, less awake!

On the other side of the scales, there is also a huge potential in shamanism, working consciously with the inforealm for the highest good of the community and the individuals within it who are seeking help, advice or healing.

In London the minority of white, middle-class British clients who come to me asking specifically for shamanic healing have usually tried many other treatments already, often including psychotherapy and anti-depressants. They would not normally go for energy or shamanic healing but they are attracted to me because of my own background and my ability to provide the scientific validation of the new field they are stepping into. Many of them see complementary therapy as a last resort when all else has failed to deal with the causes of whatever malaise is impacting their lives. They recognise that they want help and that something needs to change in their lives. Despite all the work they've done, all the treatments they've tried, they still feel blocked or stuck. Often there is a repeating pattern that goes around and around. They know their story well as they have told it many times, but it seems like each time they tell it, it limits them more as this action of re-telling embeds it deeper in the neural networks of their psyche.

I hope that this book will provide further evidence for therapists to be able to explain what is happening to their clients within Era III healings. I also hope it will persuade more people that integrating complementary therapy within a complete treatment programme is necessary in many cases, perhaps in conjunction with Western medicine, perhaps as a preventative before Western medicine becomes necessary. But it is necessary for all those who want to bring long term healing into their lives.

I can only describe some of the shamanic procedures that clients may experience if they come to me and I emphasise that the following should not be considered representative of shamanic healing with other practitioners. My practice is heavily dependent on the techniques that Alberto Villoldo teaches within the Four Winds,[88] but I have also worked directly with a number of other shamans in Peru from the

---

[88] http://thefourwinds.com

Qero and other tribal lineages. I try to work holistically, using whatever tools seem appropriate for the individual client that I am with at the time. As a result, I often incorporate more specific body work (including talking to the individual body parts, tantric sexual exercises and yogic breathwork) than would be offered by many other shamanic healers. That's why I am calling my personal healing service *Temenos Touch*, to try to make clear to people that it is a weaving together of a wide range of tools and techniques, rather than something they may have experienced before.

In this chapter I focus on some specifically shamanic tools and exercises, most of which are ideally engaged in with a qualified shamanic practitioner. One of the huge advantages of these practices is that they often work very fast and deep. They are truly for those who want to embrace change.

Illuminations to release blockages and repeating patterns

Most often in my first shamanic session with a new client, we start with an illumination, which is one of the techniques that Villoldo teaches. This is appropriate if clients have a repeating pattern, block or limiting belief in their life. I start with a brief entry interview, asking about what they would like from the session, what is the issue they want to work with and what is their intention? We decide on the name for the block or limiting belief that is holding them back or the key phrase that triggers that block for them. Then I open the healing space calling in the six directions (South, West, North, East, earth and sky) and the archetypal qualities of those directions.

Then the client lies on my massage table and I go to their head and hold under the occiput, at the limbic brain centre, asking them to breathe in through the nose and out through the mouth. With the in-breath I ask them to acknowledge the times they have suffered from this issue and with the out-breath I ask them to imagine that suffering leaving from the cells and from the energy field along with the breath. They continue to do this, gradually going back in time, allowing whatever feelings and memories of their suffering to arise. Sometimes these memories will be consciously known and at other times they come from the deep unconscious: from the inforealm. The intention is for the client to track back in time to the source of the limiting belief that is keeping them stuck, which may be in this lifetime or earlier.

Seeing the core wound, the source of our limiting belief, often allows us to release it. The process may show us that what we were conditioned to believe is not 'the truth' and that the person who told us we were not good enough, were ugly, worthless or stupid, was not acting from love or honesty, but from their own fear, neediness, damage or desire to have power and control. Just this observation often opens the door for us to behave in a different way from this moment forward. The limbic attractors can be reset.

Other times we see that we adopted the belief of someone else, to try to please them or make them feel better, but it is not our own truth. It belongs to them, not to us. This acknowledgement allows us to let this belief go and instead honour our own truth and our own path in life.

Tracking back may also allow us to see that we have tried to carry pain on behalf of someone we love, taken on another's pain to try to ease their burden, but it does not really belong to us, it belongs to the other. An example of this is the child of a parent who is ill, depressed, alcoholic or addicted. The child may step into being the responsible adult, whilst the adult takes the characteristics of being the needy child.

Or if someone has been thrown out of the family and excluded from the system, another family member may take on their characteristics to ensure they have a place, a representation in the system. Again this observation may allow us to hand the burden back to the person it truly belongs to, which often involves handing back self-responsibility, rather than trying to rescue them out of love, which has a tendency to keep the other as a victim.

During this work I sometimes ask the client to imagine the person who gave them their limiting belief coming into the room, and then I invite them to talk to that person (whether they are currently dead or still alive). The other person is always allowed to respond: what do they want to say to the client after hearing what has been said to them? (In this respect the technique resembles Gestalt therapy). This dialogue can continue for as long as it seems to be of assistance to the client and then we thank that person for energetically joining us and imagine them leaving again.

Sometimes the core wound that the client breathes their way back to may appear to come from a past life. In this case I take them through the death of that past life character in a way that will be described in detail in the next Chapter. Again there are frequently gifts or messages from the deceased that emerge as they are recognised by the living.

When the process of releasing the blockage or limiting belief or 'heavy energy' appears to be complete, I ask for 'light energy' to come in from the inforealm to replenish and rebalance the client and their system. Then I hold the client under the lumbar spine and the heart centre, allowing them to absorb the cleansing and rebalancing that has taken place in the external consciousness into the mind and the physical body.

To help people move forward in their physical lives, after this cleansing and healing at the mythical and energetic levels, I may move into different, non-shamanic techniques. For instance I may ask them to talk to various parts of the body as already described, or come up with an affirmation, or suggest some breathwork. All of these can help to anchor the energetic, mythical transformation into the physical, mental and emotional bodies as the client moves forward in their daily life.

You could say these additional exercises take the healing from the right brain to the left brain, from the intuitive to the rational, from sensing and experiencing the healing to being able to justify, verbalise and explain it.

Soul Retrieval

Because of its power and because it can be instantaneously

life changing, the soul retrieval process is one of my favourite pieces of work to engage in, but it is not to be undertaken lightly. A soul retrieval can be a very deep and intense process and therefore it is often more suitable for people who have already done significant work on themselves and yet still remain stuck in a repeating pattern for some reason that they cannot consciously identify.

Conceptually to me the way of working in a soul retrieval has immediate and obvious parallels with the Ruppert model of trauma as discussed in Chapter 3.

In a soul retrieval, the intention is for either the client themselves or the therapist to go on a mythical journey down into the underworld of the unconscious mind, where we visit four caves:

- The cave of the original wound pertaining to the issue that is keeping the client stuck.
- The cave of the contract that the client made with life at the time of that wounding in order to survive.
- The cave of the lost soul part, to see what part of the psyche or the soul split off at the time of the wounding in order to be safe.
- The cave holding a gift with qualities that would help in the client's life right now.

On the way back from the journey we invite a creature with qualities that would be of assistance at this time to join us.

Typically this journey is fairly quick in linear time: around ten minutes long. It is simply to receive the words and the images from the different caves of the underworld, it is not to get involved in understanding 'the story'. That comes in the second part of the work, after the journey. In this second stage the client visits and works with all the elements that have been seen: the wound, the contract, the lost part, the gift and the creature, to gain a greater awareness and understanding of what happened in the past that is still impacting their life today. These mythological elements are given forth by the unconscious mind, or Higher Self, or inforealm, which wants to help us to release and heal our wounds.

The first intention is for the client to rewrite the life contract to the way they would like to live from now on. Not because the old contract was wrong in any way. We often write contracts when we have been wounded (traumatised) in order to protect ourselves. But these old contracts, written in specific and often extreme circumstances, may no longer serve us today. By holding onto them, they become limiting beliefs, and so we continue to live from the wounding of the trauma and the contracts continue to manifest in our lives after they have outlived their usefulness.

To me it seems clear that contracts are written by the survival part of the psyche as it splits after a trauma (using modern trauma therapy terminology) and they become our way of operating safely in the world. But once we are able to see the core wound or trauma and acknowledge it, we are often able to recognise that we don't need to live with these outdated survival contracts any more: the healthy part of our psyches is free to write a new contract that serves us better at this current time and place.

As Villoldo puts it with regard to the contract, '*More often than not, these pledges are made silently and honoured without discussion - or even consciousness - for many, many years. And although they may have worked well at the time of our wounding to create a sense of security in a world we deemed unsafe, they go on to become the source of our limiting beliefs about abundance, intimacy, love and success. In other words, a single soul contract will spawn dozens of limiting beliefs.*'[89]

After re-writing the soul contract, the second intention with the soul retrieval process is to reunite the lost soul part, which we split off for its own protection at the time of wounding. Frequently its qualities are things like innocence, joy, beauty, a voice. Sometimes people recognise this part but are not ready to bring it back in the first session. On other occasions they feel they would like it back but the split, lost

[89] Villoldo, Ph.D., Alberto. 2005. *Mending the Past and Healing the Future with Soul Retrieval* p.64 Carlsbad, CA, USA: Hay House, Inc.

part asks that they change behaviour first, to demonstrate that it is now safe for it to come back. In these cases a follow up session at a later date is usually necessary, to consciously re-unite the splintered off part of the soul within the psyche.

This lost soul part is not quite the same as the traumatised part within Ruppert's model of trauma, but it appears to be closely related. It is not the fear that is held by the traumatised part, but rather the qualities that are hidden away after the trauma, as it was frequently the expression of these qualities that led to the wounding.

Levine has recognised the parallels between modern trauma therapy and the shamanic techniques of old. He writes, *'The indigenous peoples throughout South America and Mesoamerica have long understood both the nature of fear and the essence of trauma. What's more they seemed to know how to transform it through their shamanic healing rituals. After colonization by the Spanish and Portuguese, the indigenous peoples borrowed their word* ***susto*** *to describe what happens in trauma. Susto translates graphically as 'fright paralysis' and as 'soul loss'.'*[90]

The gift and the creature that we are shown as we journey for a soul retrieval represent qualities that may help us as we move to a new way of being. The ritual of picturing them in our lives gives us another outside resource to assist us as we re-integrate a very wounded and delicate part of ourselves that may have been split off for decades (or even hundreds of years if the core wound was being carried in the energy field from a previous lifetime).

On the encouraging side, Villoldo says, *'Although I'm trained both in psychology and the traditions of the Laika (the Peruvian shamans), I've found that one soul-retrieval session can accomplish what may take many years to heal employing psychotherapy. This is because to recover our innocence and trust in life we must renegotiate obsolete soul contracts and discarding limiting beliefs, which happens during the soul-retrieval journey. In addition,*

---

[90] Levine, Peter A. PhD. 2010. *In An Unspoken Voice: How the Body Releases Trauma and Restores Goodness* pp31-32 Berkeley, California, USA: North Atlantic Books

the language of the soul is very different from what we use in therapy and counseling. It's rich in image, myth, archetypes, and mystery – full of poetry and magic, it speaks to intuition and love. Abandonment, fear, insecurity and childhood trauma – all of these terms belong to the intellect.' [91]

Once again this points to the speed with which change is possible in the energy field, inforealm and holonomic brain (Era III healing), rather than the pedantic pace of progress in the world of the neurological brain (Era II healing).

When I am doing a soul retrieval with a client, the first thing to decide before the process starts is whether I am going to lead the client on the initial meditative journey, guiding them to collect images from the caves in the unconscious mind or whether I am going to journey on their behalf.

Some clients are clear that they want to do their own journey, and it may seem more obvious that people should journey for themselves, because how on earth would I know what has happened to them in the past? But sometimes, particularly if people are very attached to their story, it can be more effective for me to journey 'cleanly', without expectations or preconceptions. If people have done a lot of work already, they would have done this journey for themselves had that been possible. If they haven't been able to, then it may demonstrate that they are too stuck in the story - in the existing neural pathways. In these cases it may be helpful if I journey 'out of the box' for them.

In these cases I trust that the images and information I am given from the inforealm are what is needed at this time. And of course it is totally up to the client to interpret the information I receive during the second part of the process. It is important to remember that the information from the inforealm and the journey comes in metaphors and myths. The images are not necessarily facts, they are archetypical images and emotions. It is the language of the right brain, not the left brain. How these images resonate with the client is

---

[91] Villoldo, Ph.D., Alberto. 2005. *Mending the Past and Healing the Future with Soul Retrieval* p.31 Carlsbad, CA, USA: Hay House, Inc.

what is important. And somehow they always do seem to have a clear meaning for the client, in accordance with each individual's journey and story so far.

For instance, in one case as I entered the cave of the core wound on behalf of a client, I saw a number of people with their tongues cut out. To me, the thought that this image immediately brought to mind was, *'I am not allowed to speak'*. However, when I presented this same image to the client, her immediate reaction was, *'I know exactly why they don't have tongues. There's no point in talking to me. I don't listen.'* Same image, different perception, different neural attractors.

One final and I believe important issue that I want to mention here is connected with the victim, perpetrator, rescuer triangle, which I discussed in Chapter 8. It is possible that our trauma and subsequent splitting can come from a time when we were the perpetrator, not necessarily the victim. This can be extremely difficult for some people to cope with or accept. It brings up overwhelming guilt and remorse. In these cases (as in other past life work) we may have to ask 'how many lifetimes of suffering do we need in order to forgive ourselves?' At the same time, acknowledgement of core wounds that we are still carrying from lives where we did significant damage to others can lead to dramatic healing and letting go of the past, with recognition that we have atoned enough.

Case study: Harriett

Harriett works for an NGO that deals with humanitarian crises, and in her job she is taking on a huge amount of the pain of the women she works with. She feels constantly exhausted. She journeys for herself and in the cave of wounds sees a woman being raped and abused by a man. When we re-visit the scene in the second part of the session, she can't get in touch with the woman. The woman won't speak to her. I ask if the man will speak to her and she suddenly looks at me with amazement and then horror. She realises that in that lifetime she was the abuser, not the abused. What she is 'stuck' with in this life and which is leaving her completely drained is the guilt and remorse carried over from that previous life.

For her, seeing that the contract to help abused women comes from a life as a perpetrator is an amazing revelation that allows her to start acting in a very different way, not trying to absorb everyone else's suffering and so becoming much more effective in her role with less illness and more energy.

Case study: Ines

Ines is an immigrant to the UK from a culture that is very abusive to women. Looking in a mirror she doesn't recognise herself. It is hard to look and see who is there. She feels overwhelmed at work, in a very responsible job, and feels she won't be heard if she speaks out. She is suffering from panic attacks and feels like she is going to fly apart into pieces. In relationships she gives everything away, because 'that's what women do'.

We do a soul retrieval and the process takes her to a past life where in the cave of the core wound she was a female perpetrator against women, acting under orders from men. Her contract after that was, 'I have no rights as a woman'. I ask her how long does she need to suffer and hold onto that contract. She realises that she had decided to come back as a woman and suffer for as many lifetimes as the number of women she had hurt as the perpetrator. But she has done enough! Her new contract was 'I will be honoured as a woman and I will honour other women.'

That perception of the wound and the contract she has been living by for many lifetimes is an instantaneously life-changing recognition and experience.

Death rites or re-birth within life

The shamanic death rites are a healing ritual that can be started with someone who is nearing physical death and then they are completed as soon as possible after death. The Four Winds helps to run a website for conscious dying[92] by those nearing the end of their lives in the current physical body.

Alternatively these rites can be given within life when someone wants to have a metaphorical death and re-birth, when they want to completely let go of the past and bring in a

[92] http://www.dyingconsciously.org

new beginning.

The death rites are for those people who want to work in 'ayni' or right relationship. Within their own personal growth and development they are at a place of recognising that they start each day anew, and want to leave nothing unfinished at the end of each day. For who knows, that night that person may die.

We are all potentially in this world as creators, capable of choosing to live the change, helping to make things happen. When we step into ayni we have acknowledged that what happens depends on the position and attitude of the observer. It is that observation that collapses the wave function of possibility, of potential, to bring one particular scenario into being. We look at all possibilities, not just the most likely. It is the work we do in the non-physical world that manifests in the physical.

If we live in ayni we are living our truth, authentically, living with the consequences of our actions, living the way we want the world to be. That was always the traditional role of the shaman, helping to create a better future for their tribe.

When it is a death and rebirth process within the current physical body, the intention is to go through the death experience, saying goodbye to everything we have as if we are going on the journey beyond death today. We want to ensure there is nothing left undone, that could have been said, could have been acknowledged, could have been healed.

So, who would we specifically like to call in to speak to before we pass on? One by one, we invite all those that need to be spoken to, to enter the room energetically. When I do this process the client says to each of those called in whatever needs to be said to heal any hurt or wounds before they die, to voice anything they have never been able to voice in life, to tell them anything they have never dared to say or tell.

As shaman within this process I sit in the place of the person being spoken to and I may get very strong emotions and responses coming from the inforealm. If that happens then I tell the client, 'representing this person, I am feeling…', or 'representing this person, I want to say to you…'. I allow the dialogue to continue as long as necessary with each person, then I come back to myself and ask the client who they want to call in next, so that I can step into that next role. This process has many similarities to the constellations method of working with the ancestors that I discuss in Chapter 12.

After everyone that the client wants to talk to has been addressed, I count down the client's breath to their death from this current body, then invite the client's energetic aura to detach from the physical body to be cleansed in the inforealm. After a couple of minutes, because it is an exercise during life rather than real physical death, I call the cleansed energy body back and ensure it is reconnected to the physical body.

The intention is that, were the client to die immediately after doing this work, this life would be at peace. I truly believe this work is not just for us personally doing the session, but for the people we call into the room to connect with and set things right with and for the lineage, both backwards and forwards, but I will discuss this thorny belief in much more detail in Chapter 12.

Having gone through death, the next part of the exercise is the re-birth. Now that we have reached closure with the past, it is important to consider what we want to manifest in the future, in this lifetime, from this moment onwards.

To help with that when I am working with a client, I place my mesa on each of their lower four chakras in turn asking that the mesa connect with the lineage of healers to help to inform the chakra and the client.

After the words and the images and the intentions have bubbled up at each chakra we start at the root again and I repeat what the client wished for, as they themselves hold my mesa at each chakra in turn, allowing that new way of being to sink into the physical body from the energetic field.

This proves to be a profound and life-changing exercise for most of the people I have been honoured to have shared this work with. But it is not an introductory exercise, it is something to be done when the client has already done a lot of specific shadow work and is ready to move to a different level of ayni, from a wider perspective.

Sorcery, entities and psychic daggers

I mentioned near the opening of this Chapter that there is a fine line in shamanism between what in South America are called the curanderos (the healers), and the brujas (the sorcerers).

Some of my clients come from societies where shamanism and sorcery or black magic is still commonly used, and then they may come to me because they feel as if they are under attack from someone who wishes them ill. Much of Western Era I medicine would say that this is ridiculous, and some doctors would send any patient who expressed this belief for psychiatric assessment.

Whether you believe the perceived psychic attack is real or not, I have already described the power of our beliefs to impact our health. My clients totally believe in the power of the witch doctor or shaman to harm them, and as a result of that belief they react accordingly when they know someone in the community or family has been to see the bruja to ask for something bad to happen to them. Sometimes they may not know what is going on, but they have an unexplained bad feeling or sickness so they suspect a 'psychic dagger' is embedded in their energy field, even if they don't necessarily know its source.

On a personal level, I **do** believe in the power of the psychic attack, partially because I too have felt as if people were sending me negative thoughts or attempting to drain my energy at different times. Most of us have felt at some time in our lives that someone is 'out to get us' or is sending us bad luck or ill wishes. This can be perceived as a curse on the family, which in many cultures is believed to last for seven generations. I have felt a difference when that negative energy has been removed by a shaman or that cord to someone else allowing them to take energy from me has been cut. That cleansing has sometimes come from a purging through taking plant medicine, or through another shaman sensing the energetic implant and opening my energy field to extract it from me.

However, for those of you that find this a step too far, the Era II placebo effects of removing these daggers or darts from a client's system and giving them protection tools to use in the future, cannot be discounted. And maybe I too was simply reacting positively to a 'treatment' for something that was never real when I felt as if I had been cleansed of psychic attack. I can definitely report that the work helped me to feel better and regain my strength. That much was real.

And I can report that when we do this work, the other person that is sending the negative thoughts and bad wishes also seems to feel the change in how we are interacting with them, even although they don't know the work is being done.

There was one person that I had suspected of sending me jealous, damaging thoughts. I had cut them out of my life as a result. When I was in Peru in December 2012 a shaman extracted a psychic dagger from me and I suspected it had come from that person. The shaman went on to cut the cord to that person and seal it so that they could no longer take energy from me. The next time I ran into that individual was as I was writing this book in 2014, about eighteen months since I had last been in contact with them. Out of politeness I asked them how they were. They told me that December 2012 had been the low point of their life. They felt as if all their energy had gone. Co-incidence? Perhaps. But there was no way that they could have known that a shaman in Peru was cutting my energetic cord to them at the very time that their energy seemed to plummet. And I was not doing it to wish them ill. I was only doing it to stop them from draining my vitality.

Before you dismiss all this as too weird and primitive, coming only from tribal cultures, let me repeat: **many of us are indulging in sorcery on a regular basis** as we transmit negative thoughts outwards to the inforealm or holonomic storage field. We may not believe we are truly hurting people, but our underlying intention is malicious when we have cruel and hurtful thoughts. We send psychic daggers when we wish ill on an ex-partner or friend. When we say or even think things like *'I hate that stupid bastard. I hope he suffers like he has made me suffer!'* Or, *'How dare she dump me, she's such an arrogant bitch. I hope her next boyfriend dumps her!'* This energy vibrates into the inforealm where it is stored and then can be picked up and taken into the recipient's energy field leading to genuine distress. It is particularly likely to resonate coherently when the two people are still connected by the energy cords that grow within family entanglements or close relationships, romantic or professional.

If you have a difficult time accepting this then consider it from the opposite point of view. Do you believe in the power of prayer, of sending good wishes, good luck or forgiveness? That is effective exactly because of the same sort of energetic transmission which can have a profound and tangible effect whether the recipient is present and aware of your words and thoughts or not.

A less common sensation for people is that they have a live spirit attachment. They feel as if they are haunted in some way, or carrying something that is encouraging them to behave in a way they don't like. Often clients tell me that as soon as they come into my room, if that is why they have decided to come to see me. Again, for the most part I believe them,[93] and when I start to work with them I can usually sense that second energy that is not truly theirs but is hanging out in their energy field.

In my limited experience these attachments most frequently seem to be the souls or spirits or energies of people who have died very young or very unexpectedly. These souls had no time to prepare to transition to another form from their physical body. These spirits don't really recognise that their physical bodies are dead and hence they look for another live physical body to attach to. That however is not where they are supposed to be. They need to realise that they are no

---

[93] When people are starting to feel an array of entity attachments, visit after visit, there may be an issue of mental health that needs to be addressed differently.

longer in a physical body and move on from that lifetime in which they are energetically stuck on the earth plane.

Case Study: Jackie

Jackie works as an accountant and feels blocked and under psychic attack. Someone that she used to know openly cursed her and wished her dead and she feels that curse is affecting her whole family. She feels very weak and can't seem to move forward in her life.

I start with an entity extraction. Jackie is trying to cough it out, so I put an extraction crystal into her mouth and remove the entity that way. She then spits and vomits a bit more and starts crying with relief because she can feel it has gone.

I check the rest of her body for psychic daggers and both feet feel as if they are nailed down. No wonder she feels she can't move forward! I extract both of those nails from her feet. We do some further body work and I show her a way of protecting herself in the future from any other psychic attack.

At the end of the session she felt amazing and looked really strong and radiant.

On very rare occasions people may not mention anything about an entity to me, but when I tune into their system I clearly feel that there is something attached to them, which does not belong to them. In those cases I am very careful about what I say. I have to stay within their belief system and I don't want to scare them, but ideally the entity is extracted from their energy field into a clear quartz crystal within the session and then released in a fire ceremony once the client has left. As I do the extraction from the client into the crystal I acknowledge the entity's pain and suffering, but I also tell them that they are not supposed to be attached to a physical human form at this time. As far as I am concerned these entitites are not evil spirits in any sense, they are souls or energies that have got stuck in the wrong place. Afterwards I invite the energy to go from the crystal to the light, the fire or the earth, wherever they truly need to be in order to move forward to another realm or lifetime.

This process can have a very immediate and profound impact for those client who feel they have an entity or energy attached to them. During the process that entity or energy is acknowledged and separated from them, after which they feel free to be themselves.

Chapter 11: Past Life Regression

'There is a wide array of evidence for past-life experiences, but the evidence does not guarantee a correct interpretation. Spiritually disposed persons tend to assume that these experiences are from a previous life, yet this is merely one interpretation. The interpretation that is more consistent with what we know of the in-formed universe is that our brain becomes tuned to the holographic record of another person in the vacuum. 'Past life experiences' signify the retrieval of information from the A-field, rather than the incarnation of the spirit or soul of a dead person.'[94] (Ervin Laszlo)

I have had many communications from the inforealm that have appeared to be past life memories. My belief is that journeying to re-visit those lives has been of great assistance in helping me to cast aside limiting beliefs in this life and move forward. I have also worked with many clients who appeared to be carrying trauma from past lives and who have been able to change their lives significantly when they recognised ancient wounds and contracts with life. However, as Laszlo points out in the quotation above, maybe the memories are not ours.

That may well be the truth, but it still leaves open the question of why we pick up the particular information that we receive? Why is it **that** vibration that we have resonated with? Given the earlier observations from Sheldrake about the most direct and evident resonance being with ourselves, science does leave open the possibility that we are connecting with a past life of our own. But maybe not. Maybe we are tuning into something/someone else that desperately needs

---

[94] Laszlo, Ervin. 2007. *Science and the Akashic Field: An Integral Theory of Everything* p.124 Rochester, Vermont, USA: Inner Traditions

healing – a strong cry fofr help from the inforealm. Maybe it is one of our ancestors. Maybe we are tuning into a strong signal from the tribe or the society we live in. Thought forms and belief systems have energetic signatures. All religions, philosophies, sciences, lineages and cultures have signatures that we may resonate with. Whomever, or whatever the source of the waveform, that is what has arrived from the inforealm as we entered the Era III healing space, resonating somehow with our system. That is what is requesting healing.

For the purposes of this Chapter I am going to assume that we **do** have a continuing soul, and that it is our own energetic signal that we tune into, through time. This is my personal belief system and it is how I work with the many clients who share that belief system. But even if this is not the truth, this Era III work to connect with someone or something requesting healing from a different time and space still seems to have merit.

I am not officially qualified as a past life regression therapist and I don't deliberately regress people into a past life. However I have taken several Deep Memory Process (DMP) training workshops with Roger Woolger and his colleagues.[95] Woolger himself died in late 2011 and I didn't continue with the training, but I have also experienced past lives though other processes including re-birthing, work at The Monroe Institute and my shamanic training. I gained huge insights from all these experiences and some of the techniques I use in my work today come from Woolger's courses whilst others come from the other therapists with whom I have done my own past life work.

Although I don't start with the intention of regressing a client to a past life, often as I am tuning into the system, I get a sense of the time frame of any pain or blockage. It may present as being from an injury, accident, loss or stress in the recent past, it may be from much earlier in this life, it may be from birth, it may be from in utero, or sometimes it presents as being much, much older, suggestive of a past life

---

[95] http://www.deepmemoryprocess.com

experience that is still impacting the life today. Again this may not be a fact, it may be the symbolic way the unconscious has chosen to communicate something that is deeply repressed.

Sometimes as a client during an illumination journeys back to the core wound of the block that is keeping them stuck, the source of the repeating pattern or limiting belief, they may get visions that they don't recognise at all, that seem to be from a previous life or at least a previous time.

In any instance where something seems to be arising from prior to this lifetime, I ask the client to use the breath, in through the nose, out through the mouth, and count down from five to one. Then I ask them to imagine they are looking down on the body at the time of the core wound. Can they see it? Going into that body, can that person see – is it dark or is it light? Is that person standing or lying down? If they are lying can they feel what they are lying on? Can they move or are they hurt? Are there other people there? Inside or outside? Are they a man or a woman? Are they a child or an adult? Sometimes I don't need to ask any questions as the information just pours out of the client as they step into the energy of that Past Life Character (PLC). I simply need to listen and hold the space and encourage them forwards through the story that the unconscious is communicating to them.

The character may be in the middle of a trauma, or the trauma may already have taken place, in which case I ask for the breath to take them back a little further, to the time when they were hurt/abandoned/kllling or raping someone or whatever it is they were doing. What was the trauma?

The important thing in all the sessions I have done and from all the teachings I have had is then to move forwards, seeing the trauma and moving through it to the end of that life, which might be the direct result of the trauma or may be years later. Ask the breath to take the PLC to the last few breaths of that lifetime. Count down to the last breath and then see the spirit leave the physical body. As the spirit looks down it can see everything. It knows everything.

Some of the key things from that place of all-seeing and

all-knowing seem to be:

1. How was the dead body treated? Was it honoured or dishonoured? If the latter then it often seems to be very important to revisit that dead body and give it an appropriate recognition and ceremony: whether that person would have liked to have been buried, burned, put in the water or whatever. I will then do a ceremony with the client of acknowledgement, honouring and listening.

2. From the bardo state, i.e. between lives, with the guides or the ancestors or the power animals, is there anyone that the spirit of the PLC would like to call in to talk to? That might be a perpetrator, a victim, a beloved, parents, children. Allow that dialogue to unfold, giving the PLC a chance to speak, but also allowing those called in to respond to what the PLC says. This allows resolution between the various characters in the past life story.

3. What would that PLC like to say to the client in the room at this time? And what would the client like to say to the PLC? What is still being carried? What needs to be done for the PLC? What needs to be released as it has been carried for long enough?

Other ways into a PLC apart from asking the client to look down at the body include me repeating the key phrase for the limiting belief several times and asking the client to use the breath to go back to the scene of the limiting belief. What is happening there? Then I proceed as before.

Or maybe as I work in the present time, either the client or I get a sense of something happening, such as a rope around their neck or a bullet in their back. That image or sensation can be used as the entry point for a regression to the core wound, however long ago it occured, and I ask the client to focus on that story, pain or sensation and see what is happening.

I have had some profound personal experiences with this type of work, and have seen intense experiences and subsequent healing with clients. The treatment of the body after death is not always important. Sometimes people today are not concerned about what happened to that body. But when it was not correctly treated at the time of the death, then there is often a huge shift after an honouring ceremony.

In one personal experience demonstrating this, I went to a therapist as I was suffering from a physical pain in my right shoulder. As they worked with me I regressed to a past life where I felt that I been killed on the battlefield and the machete in my right hand was still raised. As I went through the death I got the vision that I had been a warrior of some kind and after I had been killed my body had been thrown into a mass grave with my companions. I didn't mind that I had fought and died on the battlefield – that had been honourable. But I was full of rage and pain that my companions and I had been dishonoured in death. As I did a ceremony to acknowledge the body and give it a proper burial I sensed that all the women of the tribe had been attached to the earth plane since that battle. They were keening and searching continually for their men. They could not go to their rest until their men had been given a proper burial.

As the therapist and I worked to give that man acknowledgement and burial, with cleansing and flowers on the grave and music, it seemed as if all the women of the tribe and all his comrades that he had been thrown into the pit with were also seen and hence allowed to move on from their stuck place on the earth plane.

And my shoulder felt better afterwards.

I have had similar experiences with clients.

Case study: Karin

Karin is another shaman who has asked me for a healing session as she has been ill recently. We start with craniosacral therapy, but as soon as I start working with her she goes straight to a past life that she is already aware of. She was a woman who suffered the loss of her entire family during a time of mass genocide. She was shot with her baby and thrown into a mass pit. Re-visiting this past life we take the baby out of the mass grave and care for it, wash the woman's body, then she takes her current day shamanic mesa and herself visualises her past life character and all the other women and children who were unceremoniously thrown into the pit with her going up to the light, honouring their suffering and allowing them to leave the earth plane.

Is it all imagination? Truthfully, who knows! And do I care? As long as it brings healing then actually no, I don't. The story is not what is important to me, the outcome is what is important. What I say to my clients is that I accept and work with whatever comes up. We all have fertile imaginations that could conjure up a million scenarios. But **one** of those millions of possibilities emerges in the session for some reason. Is it the truth? Maybe it is. Even if it is not, **that** is the scenario that comes to mind rather than any of the potential others, therefore it has an unconscious resonance with the truth that we are seeking. It is the metaphor or archetype that the unconscious has chosen to communicate with. I ask my client to work with it and trust that it is what needs to be seen at this time. It is the healing that needs to take place for ourselves and for all those we interact with in the journey.

One of the things I have touched on already is that we are all capable of being victims and perpetrators. In the Deep Memory Process courses that Roger Woolger and his team used to run, they asked participants to draw up a list of the past lives they were aware of, divided into six categories: male perpetrator, male victim, male rescuer, female perpetrator, female victim and female rescuer. If one of these categories were empty for a participant, they would ask that person to go into the next regression exercise with the intention of seeing a life within that empty cell.

Some of the people on the course found that incredibly hard. They did not want to accept that they had been perpetrators, or perhaps a man, or perhaps a woman. But when we see and acknowledge what we have done in the past, how can we judge others for doing the same thing now or in the future? If we are to fully love ourselves, we need to forgive and accept ourselves for all we have done. That then allows us to love and accept and forgive those same actions in others. That is really important, both for our own healing and to allow us to live with compassion for all people.

Case study: Lisa

Lisa has been suffering chronic migraines for the last few years. She has seen doctors and specialists and has had all manner of tests, but they can't find any physical cause of her pain. She has been referred to a pain management clinic and prescribed both anti-depressants and anti-epileptics, but she doesn't want to take them.

As soon as I tune in at the skull I feel a deep imbalance between the left and right hand sides with the left hand side feeling very heavy and inflamed. She is really surprised because as she focuses on the two sides separately she can feel the difference very clearly, but no one has ever asked her which side the pain is in, and she has never thought to focus on the two hemispheres separately.

She says she is afraid to let the pain go by releasing it from the throat chakra because if she starts to go into the pain in order to release it she will be overwhelmed. I recommend she should start listening to hemi-sync music to help balance the two sides of the brain.

On the next visit she has started listening to hemi-sync but has also started taking the medications at a low level because the pain is so severe that she can't function at work. As I tune into the system she immediately goes to a horrible vision of a past life when she was a man who had abused many women. I ask her how long she is going to punish herself? She doesn't have an answer but leaves to reflect on that vision of being the perpetrator.

The next time I see Lisa she is off all her medication and is doing much better physically but still feels depressed – she feels so much of the pain of the world. We do the tantric exercise (that I describe in Chapter13) around feminine forgiveness of the masculine. As she lists all the horrible things men have done to women and as he apologises on behalf of all men she is weeping. Afterwards she feels a huge release, as if a huge weight has been lifted off her, and she understands that she is starting to forgive herself for her past life as an abusive man. The male apology means so much to her, and for the first time in this life she feels men's Higher Self!

In Villoldo's training he asks participants to visit three PLCs:

- The life where they did the most harm or most abused their power.
- The life where they were of the greatest service.
- The life where they suffered the most.

These again are like archetypes, and he believes that if people can acknowledge and clear those three lives, the energy of the others falls like a pile of dominos. This approach prevents all of us from having to revisit potentially hundreds of past lives.

I have also done the Lifelines soul retrieval course at the Monroe Institute. They take quite a different approach whereby PLCs can get stuck in a 'bardo state' between reincarnations. They believe that each person's personal bardo largely reflects the belief system they held in life. As a result, if you believe you are going to go to hell because you have sinned, then your soul can end up stuck in a personal hell for a long time, without moving on. If you believe you just die and that is it, your soul can get stuck in a tomb, or the water after drowning, or the car that crashed, for a long time after death, without moving on. If you die after being poisoned, or drugged, or anaesthetised, your soul can get stuck in a limbo that is neither life nor death.

In these cases from your present life you need to work with the PLC's belief system. Who needs to forgive that PLC to allow them to move on? Is it God, is it their victims? How long do they need this to continue or how much do they have to suffer? Can they look down with a conscious part of the Higher Self and see the spirit leave the dead body? When that has been acknowledged then it appears that the soul can move on to another life or another place.

Finally in this and other ancestor or entity work I sometimes come across a PLC that doesn't acknowledge that they are dead. In this case I ask the client to experience what the spirit of the PLC is feeling, but also I keep asking the spirit to look down at the physical body of the PLC. What do they see happening to the physical body at the same time as whatever feelings and emotions are arising? In this case they may once again need to 'relive' the deathbed to allow the spirit to acknowledge the death from that physical body, thereby allowing it to move on and stop 'haunting' the earth plane.

So, as we enter the Era III healing space my suggestion is

to suspend belief, suspend thinking that we know the answers, the story or 'the truth'. Trust that whatever comes from the unconscious, the inforealm, the holonomic storage field, it comes for a reason, emerging from the vast array of possibilities that the imagination could contrive. Allow whatever arises to be seen, to be heard, to be acknowledged and to be offered healing. This is truly transpersonal work and gives Era III healing a much wider potential than simply one person at a time, as I discuss further in Chapter 12: Working With the Ancestors.

Chapter 12: Working with the Ancestors

'We do not yet know how a process such as a constellation, the resulting possible enlightened clarity, embodied experience and transcendent shift, affects or changes our neural connections, or helps to increase the neural connections made. We do know that sometimes experientially we engage in something that 'changes our life'; that in all of the time of ongoing therapy, or repeated constellations there may be one or two such moments that truly 'change everything'.[96](Vivian Broughton)

The shamans and many of the indigenous people have always retained a close relationship with their ancestors. More recently in Western psychotherapy the constellations framework has emerged and is now increasing dramatically in scope, stemming from the 1980s and the incredibly brave and insightful work of Bert Hellinger. Exactly how it works is still unclear, but there is now a huge experiential database from this approach over the last thirty years in what Hellinger termed 'the knowing field'.[97]

The theoretical framework of constellations is a systemic way of working, involving not only the client in isolation, but their whole system. It started with family constellations, looking at the client in the wider context of their lineage and in particular the family's dark secrets, the skeletons in the cupboard which cannot be discussed and the family members who have been ostracised and excluded.

---

[96] Broughton, Vivian. 2010. *In the Presence of Many* p.64 Frome, Somerset, UK: Green Balloon Publishing

[97] For just one book citing many references to the impact of this work, see Franke, Ursula. 2003. *The River Never Looks Back. Historical and Practical Foundations of Bert Hellinger's Family Constellations* Heidelberg, Germany: Carl-Auer-Systeme Verlag

Constellations are usually done in a group setting of around twelve to twenty people, with a facilitator and one person at a time as client. In a family constellation the others in the group are there to serve as representatives for the client's family. After a short discussion between the facilitator and the client, the client is asked to choose a representative for themselves and representatives for all initially necessary members of the lineage. These representatives from the circle of participants are invited to stand in the knowing field. As the constellation evolves it may also be necessary to bring in additional family members or representatives for people that someone in the family has wronged or become entangled with.

If you have never experienced standing in as a representative in a family constellation it may seem impossible to believe you would get meaningful information about someone you know nothing of, but often there are dramatic reactions as soon as people stand in the space of the knowing field. I have witnessed people just lying down on the floor and feeling immobilised when they are placed as a representative. At other times I have seen people experiencing acute pain in certain parts of the body, people feeling they have to distance themselves from one or more of the others in the circle and a host of other physical and emotional reactions. When the client knows anything about the person being represented, these reactions from the representative almost always turn out to have been highly accurate.

Right from the moment I came across it, the knowing field of the constellations language seemed to me to be exactly the place that the shamans have always accessed to connect with the ancestors outside linear time. A number of other therapists have recognised and started to write about the similarities between the shamanic and constellations approaches, which are simply using different labels for the same work.

For instance Francesca Mason Boring is a native American healer who relatively recently discovered constellations. She writes, *'As a Shoshone and bicultural woman,*

I have a sense that many of the links that modern people yearn for in the quest for a shaman are available in the therapeutic discipline of Family Constellation, when it is facilitated in a phenomenological way. The phenomenological approach in Constellation work utilizes the worldview that the shaman integrated with ease. It involves a way of seeing solutions using information beyond our normal objective reality. This phenomenological way of working does not involve client assessment, treatment plan, and intervention. Rather, it involves waiting, listening, and allowing an organic healing movement that comes from a field beyond the cognitive mind.'[98]

She also writes, '*these outside forces, and the participation of ancestors, were something that Native people usually talked about only among themselves, because those conversations about ancestors were among the kind of concepts that many Native people had been beaten and humiliated for.*

'*The concept of being connected to ancestors, and the dead, had been one of those areas defined as 'savage'. After a European psychotherapist, Bert Hellinger, started talking about it, some of the white world no longer thought it 'primitive'.'*[99]

Jakob Schneider, a German constellations therapist, writes, '*When there are deceased family members who are not yet at peace in the family soul, and therefore continue to affect the living as if they were still alive, the constellation work often resembles a shamanic ritual. Through the representatives, the living and the dead are able to meet, but it also seems to be that the dead can touch others who are dead. Such encounters seem to release the dead from haunting the living in their search for peace. It allows love to flow in the hearts of the living and, insofar as we can say such a thing, love also flows between the dead, and from the dead to the living'.*[100]

---

[98] Mason Boring, Francesca. 2011. *Walking in the Shaman's Shoes: A Transformational Walk with the Family Soul* ReVision 32, no.2. Sebastopol, California, USA: www.revisionpublishing.org

[99] Mason Boring, Francesca. 2012. *Connecting to Our Ancestral Past Healing through Family Constellations, Ceremony, and Ritual*, pp13-14 Berkeley, California, USA: North Atlantic Books

[100] Schneider, Jakob Robert. 2007. p.66 *Family Constellations: Basic Principles and Procedures* Heidelberg, Germany: Carl-Auer-Systeme Verlag

There are many excellent books written about the theory and practice of constellations, so here I just want to give a brief summary. This background comes largely from a constellations training course that I participated in, at which Albrecht Mahr, a close colleague of Hellinger over many years, was one of the teachers. As Mahr explains, the constellations approach starts from an acknowledgement of four levels of consciousness:

- Ego centric: everything is me, I cannot separate me and not me.
- Ethno centric, tribe centred: those who do not belong to my tribe are strangers and potentially dangerous.
- World centric: humanity is many tribes and they all matter.
- Cosmo centric: inclusive of the whole universe.
- Following on from these levels of consciousness are three different aspects of conscience:
- **Personal conscience**, which guarantees or endangers belonging to the group. It is not an absolute truth, it is a mechanism to regulate belonging. 'I have a clear conscience' implies I conform with my group's values. It is nothing to do with morality. One of the most difficult tasks facing an individual is to evolve beyond the group's values whilst still paying respect to the tribe.
- **The collective or systemic conscience of the group**, associated with completeness of the group. This takes care of and safeguards the completeness of a system. It ensures inclusion of all members and does not allow the exclusion of anybody who rightly belongs to the system. Once again collective conscience does *not* provide absolute moral orientation. It balances the integral wholeness of social groups, often by means of seemingly 'immoral' behaviour by its members.
- **Integral or spiritual conscience**, which has the capacity to move beyond duality. This level of conscience becomes extremely inclusive. This is the conscience that causes us at crucial moments to ask about our purpose.

This is the underlying philosophy from which the work

of family constellations developed as a systemic method. So, from the first contact with a client, the therapist is concerned with the client's complete family system and tribe, and the client is understood in the context of their 'soul field' that extends beyond the boundaries of the individual person.

Schneider describes how constellations work is based on the concept of entanglement within the system. *'Entanglement is what brings someone, without knowledge or choice, to repeat or blindly enter into the fate of another person in the family or group system.'*[101]

This appears to take place because, *'When a person in a family system has been excluded or denied an equal right to belong, or when someone's fate has been kept a secret (perhaps a suicide), the group conscience co-opts someone else, usually someone born later, to represent the excluded family member. This person is involved without conscious awareness and certainly has not consciously chosen to take on this task…*

'It is a process that only makes sense at the level of the soul, that is, extending beyond the limitations of time and space.'[102]

Once clients begin to work in the knowing field of the constellation and acknowledge those who have been excluded, extraordinary things can start to happen. As Schneider describes, *'There may be a powerful impact in a constellation when we become aware that some of the pain we are suffering actually belongs to someone else in the past, but has not yet been laid to rest. We are not responding to actual experiences in our own lives; we seem to be trying to be of service to those in the past, attempting to bring peace to their souls.'*[103]

Sheldrake gives one scientific explanation of how the

---

101 Schneider, Jakob Robert. 2007. p.36 *Family Constellations: Basic Principles and Procedures* Heidelberg, Germany: Carl-Auer-Systeme Verlag

102 Schneider, Jakob Robert. 2007. p.43 *Family Constellations: Basic Principles and Procedures* Heidelberg, Germany: Carl-Auer-Systeme Verlag

103 Schneider, Jakob Robert. 2007. p.13 *Family Constellations: Basic Principles and Procedures* Heidelberg, Germany: Carl-Auer-Systeme Verlag

constellation (or indeed a past life regression) might work in terms of morphic resonance *'Memories themselves do not decay at death, but can continue to act by resonance, as long as there is a vibratory system that they can resonate with.'*[104] And the holonomic theory of the brain described in Chapter 5 of course can provide the theoretical basis for a resonating field that we can connect into for information at will. We intend to stand representing someone, and by transmitting that intention and request for information outwards, we connect in the holographic inforealm with the correct information signal which with an open heart and an open mind we are capable of receiving and downloading into the physical brain.

What is crucial is for the facilitator to allow the representatives to react however they feel they want to in the space, as long as it is safe for everyone else. The skill is in holding the field, sensing who perhaps needs to be called in that is still missing, and allowing things to evolve without attempting to impose a solution.

I have been privileged to watch Mahr and Broughton, both highly experienced constellations teachers and facilitators, holding the space for a number of constellations. They work in very different ways, but both of them are really clear on intervening in the system or story as little as possible. All interventions impact the system and there is a real potential for danger when facilitators try to impose what they might like to see as a resolution.

When I was a student Mahr often said that the most important intervention of the facilitator is to acknowledge 'I don't know'. This allows the implicit knowledge and wisdom of the system to come through and express itself. The constellation is like the quantum field and contains all potentiality. Only as data is collected does the potentiality collapse to one outcome. The sovereignty of the constellation and the observation that collapses the probability wave needs to stay with the system and the inforealm, not the facilitator.

---

[104] Sheldrake, Rupert. 2013. *The Science Delusion* p.210 London, UK: Coronet, Hodder & Stoughton Ltd.

Since the ground-breaking work of Hellinger and his colleagues, the constellations approach has taken off in a wide variety of directions, including trauma constellations, health constellations, intention constellations, organisational constellations and more. The procedure and its results have grabbed the public's attention and imagination despite being very much an Era III, non-local healing method.

In the process of this rapid growth, there have been a number of splits in the constellations community. One that I want to talk about here because of its relevance to shamanism and past life regression work is the extent of the facilitator's responsibility. Every constellations therapist I have worked with or observed is clear about their intention to be of assistance to their direct client. The difference in approaches comes with respect to their intention to be of assistance, or not, to the ancestors that are called into the field during the constellation.

Some therapists explicitly believe they do have a responsibility towards all of those represented, whilst some explicitly believe they only have a responsibility to their immediate client. At one end of the spectrum some therapists believe that what comes through the representatives is 'the truth', whilst at the other end of the spectrum some believe that what the representatives feel and say is only arising from the projections (conscious or unconscious) of the client. Some believe they are bringing peace and healing to the whole system, including the dead, whilst some believe they can only change the life and health of the client in the here and now.

From dozens of constellations I have participated in as a representative and witnessed from the circle, and because of my other shamanic and past life work, my belief is that the therapist has a wide obligation when family members or others get called into the space. I believe that when a facilitator calls in an ancestor, the representative for that ancestor is accessing the inforealm. Because of that I believe the facilitator has a responsibility to that ancestor as well as to the direct client. With this belief, when the representative starts to feel the trauma of the ancestor, the facilitator needs to acknowledge this and offer the ancestor and their representative some recognition at the very least and ideally some healing or resolution. Indeed to call them in without offering this may be a direct soul re-traumatisation. The trouble of course is that constellations can then potentially become huge.

For example, imagine when an ancestor was in the trenches in the First World War and saw the horrific deaths of screaming comrades. His pain (what today we would call post traumatic stress syndrome) might never have been acknowledged or given any recognition or healing and may still be carried by the descendants. Imagine if an ancestor was raped by an invading force along with all the other women and children in her community. That tribal violation may be carried by the descendants. Imagine if an ancestor was captured and sold into slavery far from their native land after a brutalising sea passage. Again that trauma may still be carried today. So when we call in the ancestors it seems to me to be necessary to see and acknowledge their pain and suffering, and possibly the pain and suffering of those they were entangled with and died with. We have a responsibility to these souls when we call upon them. But where do we draw the boundaries of the constellation when we start to acknowledge all these ancestors and their pain?

From some of the experiences I have had and have witnessed, I believe it **is** possible that groups who died together can be helped in a communal way, just as that same group work can take place in the past life regression situation as I described in the previous Chapter. For instance the facilitator and the current family member may just need to acknowledge one of the members of the dead group and offer them assistance, and they may then be able to spread that assistance to the rest of their tribe or comrades in the inforealm.

Unfortunately however, I have observed and participated as a representative in some wider constellations where ancestors have been called in and then left potentially (re-

)traumatised because they are not really seen or offered any healing. Their pain is not acknowledged or honoured.

For example, on one occasion I stood in as a representative for someone's mother, from a culture where there has been a lot of invasion and systematic abuse of women. Almost immediately as I entered the knowing field it seemed as if I was taking on a much bigger role as a representative than just that one mother. I seemed to be touching the pain of many women in that country. The facilitator in that case was very observant of my pain and helped me to move to a chair just outside the constellations circle as she asked someone else to come in as the 'Higher Self' of that mother. As the facilitator moved me gradually further and further out, she herself started to feel physically sick and weak. Throughout the constellation I felt totally drained and disassociated from anything going on inside the circle. At the end of the constellation on that occasion the facilitator went to great pains to check in with me about what I needed in order to release that heavy representative role which she too had sensed the weight of. That was a release for me, but not a healing for the women I was representing let alone the other women of her tribe that she was energetically entangled with.

This is just one of the personal experiences that has convinced me that the scope of the work is not just amazingly powerful but also amazingly wide. In my way of thinking you need to allow enough time and space to reach a conclusion for all the representatives in the system that are called into the knowing field, not just the client.

Of course that is just my opinion and I hope that raising this debate will give rise to an informed and interesting discussion within the constellations, past life regression and shamanic communities, which appear to be quite split on this issue at present.

What does seem to be emerging at this time is that many of us are consciously stepping into the role of healing not only ourselves, with own work, but healing our lineages (genealogical and karmic) and reaching out to all humanity.

As Francesca Mason Boring writes, *'Through Constellations work, the spirits of victims who are not at rest can find peace.'*[105]

I personally know several hundred people taking on this task in their own different ways and each of those people probably knows a few hundred more. It is an incredible opportunity, but the weight of the work is enormous. I believe therapists in this space can do harm just as therapists in the Reiki space can do harm. For what do we really know of what is good for the system? We need to be especially humble in this big-picture work, stepping back from our egos. But, when done with sensitivity and care, the acknowledgement and healing of the lineages and their entanglements can also pave the way for future generations to be free of ancient karma and curses. The scope is enormous.

One of the other revelations that has emerged from constellations work as it has evolved is the extent to which many of us are carrying disease and trauma on behalf of others. What is known as the transgenerational body occurs when what has happened to the ancestors, but could not be digested, continues to have an energetic impact within the family. For instance a woman who believes she was abused by her father may actually be carrying that parental abuse on behalf of a grandmother. It is very hard to distinguish the truth and whose abuse it really is. Her father may not have been a perpetrator even if she believes he was, particularly if those memories have surfaced from the unconscious mind during therapy of some kind. Somehow the grandmother needs to be seen and allowed to speak, so that her suffering can be acknowledged and handed back to her from the current generation.

Ruppert writes, *'every time I have worked with psychotic clients I have found confirmation for an approach based on the concept of the transgenerational transfer of unresolved trauma: i.e. behind all psychotic and schizophrenic forms of behavior and experiences there are*

---

[105] Mason Boring, Francesca. 2012 *Connecting to Our Ancestral Past Healing through Family Constellations, Ceremony, and Ritual*, p.25 Berkeley, California, USA: North Atlantic Books

split-off traumatic events within the family, which the person concerned has taken on in their symbiotic entanglement with their mother, grandmother or other person from an earlier generation.'[106]

In many constellations involving ill-health, reconciliation between the client and their parents seems to be very important. That reconciliation is not to say that everything with the parents was good. It is just to admit they are the parents and that fact can never change. It is a recognition of how things were or indeed still are, such as 'I accept you are my mother and I also accept that you couldn't be there for me and nurture me as I needed.' It may include, 'I also accept that you can't be here for me now and nurture me as I would like.' This helps the client to release the constant struggle to live their life in a way that will result in their parents recognising and nurturing them. The parents simply may not be able to do that, but always trying to achieve that makes the client sick. Renunciation of the need for recognition or nurture can lead to emotional healing and better physical health.

Having seen how common carrying ill-health or other trauma on behalf of another is in the constellations setting, I have evolved a shamanic way of healing around this particular issue in the individual body work setting, using the shamanic technique of working with stones.

I place rocks on the body to represent that which the client is carrying for others. I ask the client to feel the weights of the rocks. Whose pain is this? Who does this really belong to? Sometimes if I have put on three or four rocks, the client will feel them and say, 'this one is mine, the others don't belong to me.' We can then work with who they do belong to and the client can invite that person into the room and see how they react if they are offered their own stuff back. Almost inevitably, the ancestor (living or dead) says 'thank you.' They usually say they didn't realise the client was trying to carry it for them, and they don't want that. They recognise it is theirs

---

[106] Ruppert, Franz. 2012. *Symbiosis & Autonomy, Symbiotic Trauma and Love Beyond Entanglements* p.168 Steyning, UK: Green Balloon Publishing

to carry and they want to accept that responsibility and not pass it onto the younger generations. This frees the client from being the rescuer and it frees the other from being the victim in perpetuity!

After that I sometimes bring in another, heavier stone, towards the client, asking if they will please help me, please carry this for me. Often the ability to say 'no, that is not mine, that belongs to you', is a huge moment of power, understanding and freedom for the client. They have never been allowed to say no, they have never perceived that they have choice. That permission and ability to say no and have a clear boundary of what is theirs and what is not, creates a new neural pathway instantaneously.

Case Study: Maria

Maria is 35 years old. She has done lots of 'talking' therapy, and meditates. She feels fearful a lot of the time. In particular she is fearful of anger – her own or others. If she expresses anger she will be judged and will receive anger in return.

As I work with the body she gets an empty whiteness in the solar plexus (the control and anger and stress centre of the body). She doesn't know who to put first, herself or others. Her father told her not to express herself and what she needs. I put two stones on her, one at the throat and one at the solar plexus. She feels like the one at the throat is her own but the one on the solar plexus belongs to her father. She takes it off and hands it back to her father, who thanks her.

At the throat she feels she cannot release either the breath or the anger. She just feels sadness. At this point she goes into a childlike, foetal position.

When she lies down again a little later I bring a big cushion in towards her. Can she create a boundary and push it away if it comes into her space? She is able to push really strongly, with great strength in the arms and body, but cannot say the word 'no' at the same time. She suddenly realises she cannot actually remember the last time she has said no. As she realises that, she starts to say no at the same time as pushing the cushion away, but it is really hard for her to find that voice. Her head feels afraid of being judged and of people being angry at her if she says no or doesn't please them. But she is surprised at the strength in her body and arms, the ability they have to create her own space with a boundary.

She lies listening to her heart for a few minutes before finishing. The heart feels strong, and she can feel it beating and growing. When she gets up she says she has done so much talking in the past but didn't realise how much is held in the body. She knows that is what she has to reconnect with.

Case study: Naomi

Naomi has chronic pain in one of her shoulders. I start with craniosacral therapy and there is a lot of compression and agitation in the lower spine. I move to the head and she starts getting a lot of pain all down the left hand side of her neck, arm and shoulder. I work with both shoulders and the neck for a while.

She comes again and reports that after leaving the last time she had shooting pains down the left hand side for a couple of days and pain in her feet. I again start with craniosacral therapy. Then I go to the left shoulder and bring in a rock. I ask her to think of any ancestors or anyone in her current family that carried/is carrying a huge burden. Yes, she knows exactly. Someone else in the family has suffered so much and she has tried to carry them. What would happen if she didn't carry that person any more? That person might think she doesn't love them. We talk about the victim, rescuer, perpetrator triangle a little and she starts crying – it makes so much sense to her! She keeps that person a victim and disempowers them. It is a huge revelation for her and she sees it doesn't serve either of them. She can give that person their suffering back without feeling guilty at doing so. She feels a lot lighter and more mobile in her shoulders. Her arms can move up to the side a lot further without pain.

Finally, another technique that has emerged within constellations, which can be incredibly powerful and totally in line with shamanic traditions, is to bring in a representative for time. Shamans consciously try to work outside normal, linear space and time, but people can unconsciously get stuck out there, as in those that don't realise they are dead from their physical bodies and free to leave the earth plane, or those who get stuck in PTSD, where past events are seen as present events, or those who remain entangled with the suffering of the ancestors, re-living that suffering in their current lives even when the ancestors themselves have moved on.

In these cases it can be helpful to put someone in the circle as a representative of time or as a representative of now. This can help the client to identify what is really true **now** and look back at the past from now. This can allow people to shed past terror: they are still here, in a different space and time, they have survived despite all that has happened to them and their ancestors. This can directly benefit the person who is working, but it can also allow the ancestors to be seen as they are in the present. They may now have a very different way of being, they may not still be stuck in their traumatic past. They may no longer want to be seen as victims. That perception of them is the projection of the client, not how the ancestors see themselves today.

All this work is truly transpersonal, and expands the healing potential to a much greater number of souls than those directly in therapy. This is the wide healing that Era III can offer through the generations, past, present and future. This is the work that humanity seems to really need at this time, when it is finally starting to be permitted in 'civilised societies' without punishment or ridicule. All that remains is for us is to embrace it.

Chapter 13: Sexual Wounding

'Accepting responsibility for one's own sexual needs and their consequences, and respecting the sexual self-determination of others, may require personal confrontation with the expectations of one's own family of origin as well as of society as a whole – expectations which are often adopted without much reflection.'[107] (Franz Ruppert)

I want to devote a separate Chapter to sexual wounding because it comes up so frequently in Western society. There are many different manifestations of wounding, including abuse, addiction, abortion/miscarriages, shame, guilt, longing or confusion about sexual identity. And it is not just an issue for women, there are many men also suffering from sexual wounding. These issues frequently lead to low self-esteem and a lack of self-love and acceptance.

Much of the guilt and shame people carry about their sexuality and sexual identity unfortunately stems from the variety of religions which have frequently been dominated and controlled by men and have been particularly involved in the suppression and perversion of female sexual energy and power

Christianity has portrayed the actions of Eve in the Garden of Eden as the original sin, and blame around that sin has metaphorically been placed upon all women by the Church and its representatives for over two thousand years. Within Islam women wear the Hijab because Allah has told them to cover their heads and bodies. In Buddhism the most

---

[107] Ruppert, Franz. 2012. *Symbiosis & Autonomy, Symbiotic Trauma and Love Beyond Entanglements* p.272 Steyning, UK: Green Balloon Publishing

senior nuns are considered to be junior to monks of only one day.

Regrettably certain cultures still perform female circumcision, to prevent women experiencing sexual pleasure. Women have been (and in some places still are) regarded as objects. They are frequently considered to be owned by men. Historically they have not had equal rights in many countries and they have not had any power in society, or around their sexuality: a right to say no or indeed to say yes please!

Of course some religions also prohibit sexual activity for their male representatives and devotees, leading to all the problems associated with the repression of a strong and natural human desire. Homosexuality has been outlawed by many religions and countries for hundreds of years, and in many parts of the world is still punished, leading millions of people to repress their true sexual nature. And children caught masturbating or self-pleasuring are still frequently punished in many cultures.

But of course sexual energy is one of the strongest drivers of the human condition. At the basic level we need heterosexual desire for the human race to survive. Turning the sexual act from something which in its fundamental nature is incredibly beautiful, joyful, connecting and sacred, into something sinful, violent, shameful or disgusting doesn't make the desire disappear. It just perverts the energy, resulting in the epidemic of societal problems we are facing associated with the obsessive use of pornography, rape and other forms of sexual abuse (even within relationships and families), sexual mutilation, degradation and addiction.

Tantric yoga is one of the few religions that embraces our sexual nature. As Osho writes, *'Human beings can never be separated from sex. Sex is the primary point of one's life; one is born out of it. Existence has accepted the energy of sex as the starting point of creation. And your holy men call it sinful… something that existence itself does not consider a sin! If God considers sex as sin, then there is no greater sinner than God in this world, no greater sinner than God in this universe.*'[108]

Tantric yoga calls on us all to honour all human beings as the Divine Masculine and the Divine Feminine. Then when we have sex with our sacred beloved, we are making love with and honouring the omniscient and omnipresent elements that exist in every human form. And of course if we see all of humanity as entangled parts of a greater consciousness, it makes it impossible for us intentionally to inflict pain upon another, through sexual abuse or indeed any other form of abuse such as torture or murder.

Almost every healing philosophy over millennia has concluded that it is necessary to heal and love ourselves first in order to allow us then to reach out and offer healing and love to others. And to completely love ourselves we need amongst other things to accept and love our physical bodies and our sexual energy.

For me, tantric yoga is about this acceptance. Within a relationship it invites us to allow ourselves to be truly seen, without shame, without hiding any of our shadow aspects. It allows us to use our beloved as a mirror for our faults and our fears, but also as a mirror for our beauty and our radiance.

This level of connection and intimacy (into-me-see) with another has become very difficult for most of us. It is about revealing our true selves, authentically and without fear of judgement. It is about communicating our desires clearly, including our sexual desires, which requires us to know what our desires truly are. It's about being able to say 'yes' and also being able to say 'no', knowing we will be accepted and honoured whichever answer we give.

Working like that within a relationship is a fantastic gift to yourself and to the beloved, and it's very close to my intention with clients in an Era II therapy session. I try to hold the space for the client to be truly seen and heard, with unconditional love, without judgement. But of course I am there as a therapist, not as a sexual partner and that's where

---

[108] Osho. 1973. *From Sex to Superconsciousness* St Martin's Press/Griffin, New York

the potential problem arises and why many therapeutic schools forbid touch between client and therapist. Because physical connection and sexuality have become very confused in our societies and our conditioning, the institutionally imposed 'solution' to the perceived problem is often to prohibit touch. The result is that school teachers are not allowed to hug little children who have hurt themselves. Social workers and nurses are not allowed to hug the bereaved. Psychotherapists are not allowed to touch their clients. This seems just to perpetuate the fear surrounding physical contact, yet touch is a vital part of human communication and nurturing, without which children wither away.

In Temenos Touch healing I connect very deeply with my clients at both the physical and energetic levels. That is a huge honour, but of course I have to be extremely careful to be respectful of the other's boundaries at all times, and be very clear about my own boundaries too.

For many people physical contact has been abused throughout their lives and is now associated with violence or a self-serving, grasping form of sexuality, leading them to fear any form of touch. This undoubtedly adds to the sense of alienation and aloneness that many people feel in society today, where communities and families have frequently disintegrated.

Gentle, nurturing touch can be a huge gift to people and there are many studies of the enormous benefits of massage to the elderly who may not have had any physical contact for years. But, because of society's conditioning, for some people who have never experienced nourishing physical contact, there is a danger that what body work therapists do and the way they hold the space for the work may be misinterpreted as a sexual attraction or demand. So some clients may not be ready for physical touch when they start their healing process, in which case the most important thing is for them to be able to say no, and be respected in that choice.

I want to just briefly list some of the exercises I find useful at various times for people who have experienced sexual wounding in some form.

For women who have experienced wounding in the yoni (all the sexual organs combined, incorporating the first and second chakras) I may ask them to imagine a powerful white Reiki (Universal Energy) stream of light winding around the inside of the womb, forming a healing sphere. Then I ask them to imaging wrapping that stream of light around the fallopian tubes, around the ovaries, down the cervix, the vagina, around the labia and the clitoris. Imagine allowing the healing Reiki light to come in to all those sexual, reproductive organs. And if there is scar tissue, fibroids, endometriosis, infertility, STIs or any other ill-health in the yoni, we invite the Reiki to help the body to release any cells that are not in the perfect template of health, in the safest way possible, to be replaced by cells working optimally, in the perfect template of health for the best interests of the client's Higher Self.

A very similar exercise can be very helpful for women who are trying to conceive. I suggest that before they make love, they imagine the stream of Reiki light all around the womb and the sexual organs, creating a beautiful, sacred, welcoming space that they can invite a soul to enter.

Incomplete pregnancies are another very common wound for women, arising because of termination or miscarriage. Incomplete pregnancies can of course also be a huge source of pain for men. Sometimes their partner may not have allowed them any choice or even told them about the pregnancy and they find out after an abortion has already taken place. Sometimes their partner may have made a different choice from what they wanted with respect to a termination. In the case of miscarriage the wound for the father may come from the fact that they too wanted the baby to survive and had formed a loving attachment to it.

The midwives and gynaecologists that I hear about from my clients do seem to be getting much more tuned in to the emotional pain that can be associated with an incomplete pregnancy and are much more sympathetic than they were just a few years ago. Parents are usually allowed to see their dead child and carry out some sort of ceremony to honour its passing if they wish to, but this is not always the case and sometimes people at the time of the event don't feel able to deal with a ceremony right then.

If people believe in the continuation of the soul after death and/or re-incarnation, then they often seem to find it extremely helpful, sometimes many years later, to do a ceremony for the child who was lost through the abortion or miscarriage. If I am doing this exercise with a client, I ask them to reflect on what gifts and lessons that short pregnancy brought. Then we imagine calling the soul into the room and the client thanks it for the gifts and lessons it gave them in that short time. Then we can use a prop for the baby (something like a vase wrapped in a beautiful cloth works well.) Holding 'the child' the mother or the father or both together can do whatever sort of ceremony they would like: they might like to imagine burying the child, or giving it to a fire or to water, perhaps lighting incense or candles, and placing flowers, and honouring the soul and its place in the lineage with a song, or a reading. As they do the ceremony they can give the soul whatever blessing they want for the future. Often the soul wants to make some sort of reply and of course that is invited and heard. This type of Era III healing can be hugely powerful for the parents but also for the spirit or energetic resonance of the child as it continues on into the inforealm.

Even if a client doesn't believe in an ongoing soul of any sort, then the client can still consider whether there were any gifts or lessons from the short pregnancy, and conduct a ceremony of acknowledgement and closure. But in these cases there is no forward blessing for the soul or any response from the dead child, it is purely for the Era II mental and emotional health of the parents.

Moving on to erectile dysfunction, I don't get very many clients presenting with this condition (possibly because I am a woman and men may prefer to discuss this issue with another man), and of course there may be physiological reasons for the dysfunction, in which case the client may need to see a medical doctor. But if the client is otherwise fit and healthy, the first question is whether the problem only appears in certain circumstances, for instance a man can maintain an erection and ejaculate through masturbation, but not with a partner. In this case the cause may be emotional, (such as 'I don't believe I deserve this woman') or physical (such as desensitisation through prolonged use of pornography, which in itself is probably the result of some other conditioned belief). In other cases the source cause of erectile dysfunction may be a much older issue, for instance beliefs about sex that were imprinted in childhood, inappropriate sexual contact at an early stage, or issues around self-esteem. In these cases we can work to treat the wound as with other limiting beliefs, going back to the source and working to release that conditioning from the system.

I have also come across instances of dysfunction which appear to be the result of a psychic attack. In certain cultures the negative aspects of shamanism can include putting a curse on a man's virility, in which case I work just as with any other extraction of a psychic dagger.

I had one client, an incredibly strong and healthy man, who worked out in the gym all the time and took all sorts of natural dietary supplements, but since his last girlfriend split up with him several years earlier he couldn't get an erection in any circumstance. As I held his body, it felt as if there was an iron bar across the second chakra preventing any energy from flowing down to the root. When I asked if his ex might have deliberately or otherwise sent a psychic dagger he looked astonished and said absolutely yes, she was into black magic. But he questioned whether she could really have had this effect. When I assured him that I believed so, he was incredibly relieved and we energetically extracted the bar that was blocking the second chakra and allowed the life-force to flow down into the root again.

Gender confusion and sex addiction are quite specialised areas and they are not something I encounter very often, but when I do, once again the client usually holds a core limiting belief. For instance they may feel that homosexuality is wrong, that women are inferior, that they are unlovable, or that they only escape their pain through sex. Again we work with this limiting belief or repeating pattern in the same way as with any other issue, but it is important for me to be aware if these clients are on medication or potentially self-harming, in which case I may feel it is more appropriate for me to refer them elsewhere.

Now to move on to rape and incest. Clients who have suffered from these experiences can potentially require specialist sexual counselling, with repeated incest in particular being a very entangled family trauma. It is recognised in the psychotherapeutic literature as being one of the most difficult issues to deal with, followed by rape by someone the client knew and trusted, followed by rape by a stranger. And let me emphasise again that I am not only talking about the sexual abuse of women, but also the sexual abuse of men.

In the case of incest or rape by someone the family knew and trusted, there can be huge shame and guilt accompanied by anger directed not only towards the direct perpetrators but also towards those who stood by and consciously or unconsciously allowed it to happen. I have had two clients (one man and one woman, from different countries) who as children were sexually abused by priests in the Catholic Church. Both of these children told their parents, whose response was that they should keep quiet about it. It was known of but no action was taken. In each of these cases the clients had found it possible through work over the years to forgive the priests – that was just what they did! But neither of them had found it possible to let go of the abandonment by their parents, who did not protect them from someone who was revered by a community that collectively ignored their damaging behaviour.

In cases of incest the entanglements within the family are profound. Many times the child may allow abuse from the father because they think they are either protecting their mother and/or their siblings. But there are other cases when the mother is fully aware of the father's (or grandfather's) actions and does nothing. There can be role confusion, abandonment, shame, guilt, rage and still love, perhaps even an admission of pleasure. These are cases where body work, mind work and constellations may all need to be used to help provide an integrated healing potential for the client and the wider system in order to prevent future generations from experiencing a continuation of the systemic trauma.

Often when I start working with a client who has experienced sexual abuse, I don't know that story. And I have to be incredibly careful if I want to introduce a question about it into the healing. As I hold the second chakra and feel the client's pain there I might say something like 'I sense that you have a very wounded feminine. You have been very hurt I suspect.' At that point the client may start crying or may start to talk. If they don't acknowledge any resonance with those words then the system may not feel safe enough to go to there just yet.

Some women have very persistent cystitis, which the medical profession has repeatedly attempted to treat with a succession of antibiotics, but with only temporary or limited success. This frequently turns out to be associated with sexual trauma in the past, such that any sexual relations in the present trigger the tension still held in the yoni, resulting in contraction during sex and hence the bruising that results physiologically in cystitis. Again for long-term healing the client needs to face the original trauma in a held, safe space, to allow those feelings to emerge but with a different outcome, creating a new neural pathway.

Each case of sexual wounding is very different. Sometimes the trauma needs to be acknowledged and released. Sometimes people need to learn that they can say no. Often there needs to be self-forgiveness, then self-acceptance and eventually self-love. There may be frigidity around sexual relations now, or at the other end of the spectrum some people repeatedly attract abusive relationships, and become promiscuous in the search for connection and love which they associate with sex and physical or emotional abuse. In such cases that repeating pattern needs to be broken, the cause of their actions needs to be acknowledged and a new belief and attractor pathway needs to form in the mind for healing to take place and a new way of living to arise.

One more exercise that can be incredibly powerful and healing for sexual wounding, is to allow the heart and the yoni (or the heart and the lingam, the male sex organs) to reconnect, aided by breathwork. Often people suffer a disconnection between love (the heart chakra) and sex (the first and second chakras). I quite frequently ask clients to put one hand on their heart and the other hand on their sex centre. What happens if they allow each of those centres a voice and invite each of the centres to talk separately? What does the sex centre need and desire? What does the heart centre need and desire? Is there anything they would like to say to each other? See what happens when they are allowed to enter into dialogue.

Quite often clients say something along the lines that from the heart they want to be open and trusting and loving, but from the yoni they want to be protected and respected. The yoni has frequently been objectified and heart has closed off to that pain for its own protection. It is a form of dissociation, but it is accessed by the client and therapist together through the conflict felt between different parts of the body, not through the mind, and it does not stem from parental attachment deficiencies, but from relationships in puberty and beyond. It is healed by bringing into consciousness the acknowledgement of what each part desires and allowing that to be freely expressed.

I will also invite head to respond to what the others express and of course it may have a very different view, representing the rational left brain or the survivor personality, rather than the empathic, emotional centres. As with any other form of wounding I find it is important to encourage a dialogue between all the body parts to try to bring them into a state of co-operation rather than conflict.

When that dialogue seems to have finished, I ask the client to breathe deeply and try to imagine energy pulsing up from root to the heart chakra on the in-breath, and flowing down from the heart chakra to the root on the out-breath. As they breathe, can they feel that pulsing energy connecting sex and heart?

Sometimes people may feel the energy going more easily one way than the other and sometimes they don't feel the two centres can connect at all. If they won't connect I ask the client to try to get a sense of where the blockage is. For instance it may feel as if the solar plexus is blocked or tight or has a bar across it. In this case I can work on the blocked area with visualisation: who do they feel put that block there? Was it themself or another? How does it serve them to hold onto that block? Can they release it? I may be able to extract a psychic dagger that is causing the block.

The intention is to work towards allowing the heart and the sexual organs to connect, in acknowledgement that we are in a gender determined body and that when we choose to engage in sacred sex involving both heart and yoni/lingam is our birthright.

Case study: Olga

Olga came in with a lot of anger about her previous relationship. She has done quite a lot of work on herself in the past, but she has stopped doing any healing for a while now and acknowledges that she knows part of the problem is that she is living entirely in her head these days, disconnected from her body. Her last partner treated her as a sexual object.

I start at the feet where there is very little energy. I move to the solar plexus which feels incredibly tight and angry and she does a lot of screaming, releasing some of her anger and tension. We cut the cord to her ex-partner at the root and then she puts her hand on the yoni, the first and second chakras, feeling into that part of her body. What does it want to say? It wants to be respected, to be honoured and it's not just there for everyone else.

What does heart want to say to yoni when she hears that? Heart says that is what yoni deserves, nothing else will do.

How is head? Head asks what the fuss is all about. Everything is fine! Head is also afraid that if yoni doesn't do what people ask it will end up alone.

Yoni then wants to scream at head 'that's not good enough, I have to be respected.'

I ask her to hold her own breasts and meditate on the feminine. She feels really confused. There is so much pain and disrespect around the feminine. Why do men treat us all like that? She doesn't know what self-respect would feel like. Her mother doesn't have it. Other women she knows don't have it.

I ask her to switch to having one hand on the breasts and one hand on the yoni and I invite her to breathe and circulate the energy between the two. At first she can't do that at all. There is no connection. I ask if she can recognise that she had enough self-respect to spend time, energy and money in coming to see me? Yes, she can acknowledge that. She can now start to feel the energy rising between the root and the second chakra, and coming down from the heart to the solar plexus, but there is still a gap between the second and third chakras.

We finish the session with a meditation on the feminine that she can do at home to continue what we have started during the session, acknowledging the feminine, the pain and the beauty, the abuse it has received and its power.

Finally there is a hugely powerful tantric forgiveness meditation that I use in workshops as well as in private sessions. It is usually done in pairs with a man and a woman, but can also very effectively be used for men with men or women with women, depending on the wounding that is present for those involved.

In this exercise, supposing it is a man and a woman, first of all the man sits on the floor in front of the woman, as a representative of all men. The woman tells him all the ways that men have hurt her in this life, then how men have hurt her in past lives (if she is aware of these), then how men have hurt all women in the world through the ages and continue to do so today. The man apologises on behalf of all men and offers her a humble foot massage and a flower as a token of apology. As a representative of all men he asks for her forgiveness for all the ways she has been hurt. The woman may say that she does forgive or that she is ready to start the process of forgiveness or that there are some parts she can forgive but some parts that she can't let go of just yet – whatever feels authentic for her at that moment. Then the exercise is repeated with the woman sitting in front of the man as a representative of all women, as he speaks of all the ways that women have hurt him and all men throughout time.

When this exercise is widened out in this way from the people directly concerned to all their feminine sisters or masculine brothers, it starts moving towards forgiveness of all the things that men have done to hurt women over all lifetimes and vice versa. By extension, as the feminine starts to forgive the masculine, this includes forgiveness of herself and the hurt she has caused to women whilst in a man's body during past lives. As the masculine starts to forgive the feminine, this includes forgiveness of himself and the hurt he has caused to men whilst in a woman's body during past lives. The work of healing becomes truly transpersonal, connecting with the inforealm to reach out to all beings in the past, present and future and all of humanity can benefit as this compassion and forgiveness ripples out.

As with shamanic practices, past life regressions and working with the ancestors, when we do this Tantric work deep in the inforealm we are stepping into creating a new way of living in the world, offering recognition, apology and healing to all those we are connected with through the cosmic consciousness.

Osho talks of the way love moves from self-love, to love of the beloved, to love of the cosmos. *'Falling in love you remain a child; rising in love you mature. And, by and by, love becomes not a relationship, it becomes a state of your being. Then it is not that you love this and you don't love that, no – you are simply love. Whosoever comes near you, you share with them. Whatsoever is happening, you give your love to it. You touch a rock, and you touch as if you are touching your beloved's body. You look at the tree, and you look as if you are looking at your beloved's face. It becomes a state of being. Not that you are 'in love' – now you are love. This is rising; this is not falling.'*[109]

This is the sacred sexuality and Oneness that Western

---

[109] Osho. 2000. *New Man for the New Millennium* Osho International Foundation, www.OSHO.com/copyrights

society often seems to be divorced from and which this work can help us to reconnect with.

Chapter 14: The Importance of Ceremony and Ritual

'At the level of inspiration you enrich life with your own rituals. You connect naturally with the great myths and symbols. Ritual and myth seem your natural language... Your own sense of ritual and theater can mark every day, as well as special occasions, with the celebration of spirit.'[110] (Gabrielle Roth)

Rituals have largely been lost in the Western world, and the ones that remain are mostly religious, often connected with birth and death, but there are many good reasons to use rituals much more frequently to mark many sorts of events. After shamanic and other Era III healing work, change is installed at the mythical and energetic levels, but we need to install it in the physical and mental levels too. Rituals help to connect the energetic and the physical. A different way of putting this is that change is installed in the right brain during the shamanic work and then needs to be communicated to the left brain. The ritual can be the transmission and anchoring method and the more the ritual resonates with the individual the more successful the anchoring is.

The impact of ritual comes partly from taking time out from our normal activities. We take the time to set the scene for our personal development and healing work, honouring nature or the ancestors or whatever we are working with in the ritual, making the space beautiful, using our creativity. The impact also comes from setting-out and then declaring our intentions in a witnessed, sacred space.

---

110 Roth, Gabrielle. 1989. *Maps to Ecstasy* p.197 Mill Valley, CA, USA: Nataraj Publishing

My suggestion for maximum impact is to take rituals seriously, collect the right tools, dress up, get all the necessary bits and pieces together. Engage with the ritual in your mind, your body, your clothes, your actions, your thoughts. Be fully in it. You are honouring something sacred and often ancient with the ritual, creating an energy field that beams out and connects in the inforealm, resonating with all those who have done that same ritual in the past, calling in the ancestors, calling for help. We need to make that energetic transmission outwards as strong as possible to achieve maximum resonance with the inforealm.

Because of their sacred nature and their intention to connect with the universal consciousness, it is important not to rush rituals but to give them time for the deep energies to emerge from the field. Rituals take as long as they take, they don't run to a timetable. Chill, relax and wait.

Some of the rituals that we can incorporate into our everyday lives and which I encourage my clients to use as they find helpful include:

- Let go of that which no longer serves you by acknowledging it then consciously blowing it into a stone and burying it in Mother Earth, or blowing it into a stick and burning it in a fire. This is both an acknowledgement of that which doesn't serve and then an intention to release, to let go.
- Create a beautiful space to receive rites and attunements or to meditate in. This is an acknowledgement that we are working with something special, something sacred, something that is worthy of effort because it is important for ourselves and for others.
- Acknowledge the gifts and lessons that we received from people that may no longer be in our life for a variety of reasons, then release that person or event whilst retaining and integrating the gifts and lessons. This is an acceptance of non-attachment, but also a closure ritual with blessings rather than with ill-thoughts or psychic daggers.
- Respect people's fate and don't try to carry it for them. Allow the ancestors their dignity and their choices, which

may involve giving back a burden which you have tried to carry for them.

- Allow yourself freedom to say farewell, goodbye. This is over, I am leaving now. This may include cord cutting which I discuss in more detail immediately after this list.
- Acknowledge an excluded person, recognise that they are part of your system, your tribe, your lineage. This may include bowing to them or acknowledging their role as a perpetrator, seeing their place in the system, even if it is then to cut yourself free of that system and follow your own path.
- Acknowledge a quality or a lost part and bring it back into your energy field through one of the chakras. This can be enhanced by writing affirmations, meditating, chanting mantras, drawing pictures of the qualities, using power animals as archetypal representatives of the qualities and so on.
- Conduct a ritual for the burial and release of the dead in whatever way you feel they would like their lives to be honoured.

One of these rituals is saying farewell through cutting the emotional and energetic cords that link you with another through time and space. Again if you think such a cord is improbable, you can think of it as an extension of the interpersonal neurobiology so clearly articulated by Allan N. Schore.[111] Attachment studies focus on the implicit right brain to right brain affect communicating and regulating mechanisms of intimate relationships. Why is it called 'attachment'? What exactly is the affect communicating regulating mechanism? It's interesting that if something is labelled a mechanism we accept it, but if we label it an energetic cord we dismiss it!

If a client decides that they want to cut the energetic cord to another, this is not implying that they no longer love the other, but it is acknowledging that they are not dependent (or

---

[111] For example see Schore, Allan N.. 2012. *The Science of the Art of Psychotherapy* New York, NY, USA: W.W. Norton & Company, Inc.

even co-dependent) on the other. In the shamanic way of thinking it is not healthy to have a cord connecting to another individual, as eventually it will drain one of you of energy. If you are corded to someone for a long time your behaviour can change to be like theirs – exactly as implied in the modern neuropsychology of mirror neurons and attachment theory. Cords rob us of our energy and our autonomy. Our true strength and essence must come from within, not from outside approval or support.

Cutting the cord is cutting the co-dependency, the perceived need to drain energy from another. And often an old relationship cord may need to be cut to allow space for a new relationship to grow.

Sometimes people don't want to cut a cord because the pain is the last thing connecting them to another. It's the last ray of hope, of clinging on, and that can apply to people we love and also to people that we deem have done us wrong. That is even more reason to cut them. Keeping the cord in place holds us in the past.

I have personally experienced being on the receiving end of cord cutting as well as having viewed the potentially dramatic results of cord cutting for my clients.

On the receiving end, a partner had broken up with me a few months earlier and although at the time of the split I had been devastated, I was apparently getting over it and feeling much better. Then one week I felt terrible again. I felt abandoned and rejected and had no idea why. At the end of that week my ex-partner e-mailed me to say he had been cutting the cords that had remained energetically attached to me and wanted me to know that he did not intend to stay in contact with me from that time on. That explained my feelings of abandonment and rejection, although I had had no idea during the week, as my feelings emerged, that he was doing that work!

Working with clients, I have had people whose phone has started ringing as they were in my room, or as they were walking down the road after the session. Someone they have not seen or heard from for years is attempting to reconnect, because we have cut the energy cord in the session. How do they know? Back to the inforealm!

When I am working with someone who does want to cut cords, I usually (but not always) ask them to imagine the person they want to cut the cord to coming into the room energetically. What was the gift or lesson from knowing that person that they will always have? I invite the client to voice those gifts and lessons to that person with gratitude, as I witness the acknowledgement. Then I invite the client to offer that person whatever wishes they want for them in the future before telling them that they are letting them go. They no longer wish to remain energetically entangled with the other person.

Then maybe the client knows where they feel energy draining from them to that person, or I have to sense where that is. It is typically flowing from a chakra or an organ. I open that area carefully and feel for the energetic cord. Then I give the client a knife and as I pull the cord out, I ask them to cut it as close as possible to their body. Then I drop the cord into the fire and bring in a flame and smudge to cleanse and seal the area. I finish by closing the area energetically and bringing in balancing light.

The only time when I would not call the entangled person into the room to be spoken to is when there appears to be 'black magic' or psychic daggers being sent by the person we are cutting the cord to, i.e. they are using the cord with malevolent intention. In that case I simply cut it without any engagement with them.

Within the shamanic tradition, two other rituals that I use frequently for myself and for clients are the ritual of changing perceptual state and the ritual of the fire ceremony.

As we have seen already, consciously or unconsciously we choose what we see. But if we can change the place we view events from, our understanding of the events may also shift. Within the Andean shamanic lineage there are seven perceptual states. Each one resonates with one of the archetypes, which in that tradition are serpent, jaguar, hummingbird and eagle, plus the keeper of the Lower World (our unconscious), the keeper of the Middle World (our waking world), and the protector of the Upper World (our super-conscious).

Serpent resides in the root chakra and keeps us connected to the ground. It has the quality of helping us to shed our past in one piece the way it sheds its skin.

Jaguar resides in the second chakra and helps us to track outside conventional space and time.

Hummingbird resides in the solar plexus and helps us on our soul's journey.

Eagle resides in the heart and can see the bigger, more complete picture, from on high.

The ability to see clearly what is normally suppressed or hidden is assisted by the keeper of the Lower World, associated with the throat.

The ability to see clearly what surrounds us in everyday, three-dimensional reality, is assisted by the keeper of the Middle World, associated with the third eye.

The ability to see our potential, to co-create our own destiny, is assisted by the keeper of the Upper World, associated with the crown.

A really profound exercise can be to view a major decision, a life block, a problem or hurt from each of these different perceptual states in turn. It is not that one is right and one is wrong. They are just different and will give you different possible solutions and a wider range of options than you might come up with from just one perspective.

The final ritual ceremony that I want to mention here is one that is of huge significance to shamans throughout the world: the fire ceremony. We can give things to the fire to be burned in cleansing and closure. We can take things from the fire in renewal. We can feed our energy and our healing kits from the fire. We can connect across space and time through the fire. This last is why shamans around the world, even today, hold global vigil fire ceremonies, when fires are lit and tended across the world simultaneously, usually for a minimum of forty-eight hours and perhaps for as much as a week. The fire vigil (ritual) creates a strong signal to send to the inforealm with our collective intentions or prayers for change and healing, acknowledging that these can get picked up where they are needed as they create a cosmic, resonating, coherent wave.

Part 3: Experiences

Chapter 15: Case Studies

I have integrated snippets from work with clients throughout this book, but here I give some examples demonstrating the scope of techniques that I might use with a single client over a few sessions, which in total may span a number of weeks or years. This integration and weaving together of techniques from a wide range of lineages is what I call Temenos Touch healing.

In all cases the names have been changed and details have been altered and omitted to protect the identity of my clients. In some instances two or more people may have been conflated into one case study for illustration. I have also given all the case studies female names, as an additional layer of anonymity, although in real life they represent both men and women.

Amber: Seven sessions over thirty months

1. Amber is in her late twenties and suffers from periodic depression. She is working incredibly hard, all hours of the day, to make ends meet and has the constant feeling 'I'm not good enough'.

She describes her father as a controlling, abusive man and in her life she has dated a succession of controlling, abusive men. She feels she can never say no to anything, work or sex or whatever else people want to obtain from her.

We do an **illumination** where a huge amount of anger and guilt and sadness emerge and we **cut the cord** to her father. I hold her under the heart and the sacrum and lead her into a **meditation** connecting with the power of the feminine from mother earth and the power of the masculine from the sky and the cosmic consciousness.

She feels much lighter at the end.

2. Amber announces she has started saying no to people. This time we start with the **finding your essence** exercise to release roles that don't serve her. She burns lots of the roles and realises as she looks at her life there is nothing present about her relationships with people. It's all about work.

We then do some **body work** where there is huge **unwinding** and release of tension from her spine and solar plexus.

3. She feels a bit stressed but has been putting her foot down at work, saying she can't do so many hours and taking care of herself much better. She feels she has been finding her voice and in the session itself she is able to ask for what she wants from me. We do some **body work** leading to **inner child visualisation** and then there is lots of **shaking** in her body. She feels something is stuck in her throat and then there is a huge **unwinding** in her head, neck, shoulders, back. She feels something release and then she is able to ask me to **cut the cords** to two more people that she feels have been draining energy from her.

At the end of the session she feels amazing – really light and balanced and very positive.

4. She has started to lose weight by eating better and exercising more and taking care of her body, and is feeling much more positive and less depressed.

We do some **body work** and I give her the **archetypes** in her chakras to help resource her and allow her to look at things from **different perceptual states**.

5. She is finding her boundaries and her self-respect. She won't put up with something that's not good enough any more and she can ask for what she wants.

We work intensively with her neck and shoulders, **releasing all the weight she has been carrying on behalf of others**. She recognises that she doesn't need to carry the family and all her work colleagues any longer.

6. We repeat the **essence exercise** and it is very different from the previous time. It helps her realise how far she has come and this time she brings in some really positive and powerful qualities to the centre of her life.

We move on to an exercise on **non-attachment** and then some **breathwork** with further releases of anger. Then a sense of forgiveness starts coming through and a realisation of the transpersonal. She can stand in her essence after everyone has come and gone and feels she can have her own life at last. She sees so much is possible when she steps outside her place of fear.

7. She has started dating again but is able to be selective and say no, which feels really powerful for her. She has a new job with fewer hours where she is seen as a valued member of the team. We work with the different **perceptual states** again and from the place of eagle she can see herself as a little ant scurrying around. She never wants to live in constant fear and judgement again. She feels as if she is in a really good space, able to look at herself in the mirror and acknowledge how far she has come. She feels like a powerful, attractive woman.

Bernadina: five sessions over fifty-seven months

1. Bernadina is a workaholic and punishes her body by pushing it to the limit at all times, mentally and physically. But she has recently been diagnosed with a chronic illness which she doesn't even want to name to me.

I start with **Reiki** and sense huge stress in the system – it feels really taut, jumpy, jerky, and there seems to be an energy block across the left hand side between the second and third chakras. It feels like a hard unnatural ball. I asked her to breathe down into the second chakra but she can't – she is aware of the block exactly there.

She is aware she is not kind to herself but hopes coming to see me is a first step in changing that.

2. She has changed her diet to help with the chronic illness which she can now name and talk about. I do an **energy extraction** around the area I had identified as having a block in the previous session. Then when I **hold the head** there is a noticeable **left/right split**. The right hand side feels shut down, the left hand side feels agitated. Asking her to feel

the two sides of the head separately if possible, to her the left feels tangible, she can get in touch with it, the right feels empty, light, airy-fairy!

I suggest listening to **Hemi-Sync** music as much as possible to try to bring in some hemispheric balance.

The system just feels exhausted, as if it is running on empty, and for the rest of the session as I **work on the body** she falls deeply asleep. We agree that in the next session I will give her the Reiki 1 attunement for self-healing.

3. **Reiki Attunement Level 1**

4. She reports that initially when she was doing the self-healing after the attunement, it brought up a huge amount of anger. It reminded her of her childhood and her very angry father. So she stopped. She is incredibly busy at work again so everything regarding taking care of herself has gone out the window.

I start with **Reiki** and initially she feels very grateful for being reconnected with the healing. Then she gets very sad that she is not fulfilling her purpose, or honouring herself. Just working for money. Then she starts having difficulty in breathing and I can feel her fear arising. We go back to a very early **childhood memory** which brings up a lot of sadness. But at the end she feels 'very different' and 'much lighter'.

5. She is still super-busy, but is making time for her hobbies and friends as well as her financial employment. The chronic illness is still there but medicated to be under control. However, she sees that everything she does is to the extreme – there is no middle road in anything and her life feels out of balance.

I sense into the system for a few minutes and then I put a few **small stones on the solar plexus area.** She is amazed how heavy and painful they feel. I ask her if she wants me to put more on. Initially she says yes, keep going until it hurts too much. But then she gets an excruciating pain in the lower thoracic back. 'Stop. It's enough!' **I have her feel the stones. Whose pain are they?** She immediately recognises different ones as belonging to different members of her 'horribly entangled family'. She initially says she chooses to keep them, to try to be of assistance. **I ask her to feel each one in turn and see if there are any that can be released at this time?** Gradually, sensing into each one of them she is able to take off and hand back three of them. One was to her mother who was so relieved – she never wanted her to have it. Two others were connected to people at work who received them back gratefully.

She feels better although there are some stones still there – but she chooses to keep them for the moment.

Then I bring in the biggest stone I have and ask if she would please carry it for me? She looks at me with horror and then a recognition of her habit of always saying yes. Now she is able to say no. I try to persuade her to carry it on my behalf, to help me, but she is clear – she doesn't want to and is able to say no. She is really surprised at herself and how natural it feels to say no!

Christina: five sessions over eighteen months

1. Christina, in her twenties, has lived in the UK all her life but comes from an immigrant family with a culture of shamanism. Her father has been physically present but emotionally absent all her life and she feels she needs to look after her mother and her brother. She feels she may be under psychic attack and has attempted suicide.

In the first session I do an **illumination** and also **extraction of psychic daggers**. She spontaneously went to a **past life** as a young man who had been thrown out of his village by the elders and committed suicide. His message to her was 'you don't have to do it this way.' She held her own breasts in the **breast meditation** as I held underneath her body, connecting her with the feminine energy of mother earth. As a woman in this lifetime she came up with a new **affirmation** 'I am free and I can love'. At the end she looked really happy, had gained understanding from the past life and felt peaceful, with less need to look after everyone else in the family.

2. After the last session she worked with her affirmation

and felt a huge change in attitude. She has started to be able to delegate tasks to other people. She feels much happier now.

We do the **essence exercise** and she burns most of her roles, choosing only a few to keep. She feels as if she has lots of choice in her life right now and likes stepping out of the old momentum of the roles. Finishing again with **breast meditation** for the feminine, it feels strange to her and a bit frightening to step into the feminine rather than the masculine, carer of the family role, but it's good!

3. Again she feels as if she is under psychic attack from the family's country. I get a sense of a slash wound across the top of her right leg. She feels 'very strange' sensations in her leg as I work to **extract the psychic dagger** and bring in healing. There also appears to be a metal bar down the right hand side of her face. She often feels there is something there to stop her from speaking. Again I cleanse it and her leg again feels very odd as I worked with the face. There seems to be a connection between those two psychic daggers. I give her **bands of protection** and show her how to feed them and work with them.

4. She and her family have moved to a much more supportive community but she still feels there is a block around her career. Also she feels she has taken in another entity whist she was doing healing work on someone else.

I start by **removing the entity**, then move on to **craniosacral body work**. What is she not allowed to express? Her feelings. If she does speak authentically then people get angry with her. The family operates from fear and guilt. As she says that she can feel something like a belt being squeezed around the second and third chakras, tighter and tighter and a weight and pain in her head. We **call the whole lineage of women** into the room and she hands their stuff back to them. They apologise, saying they were trying to help, they didn't realise they were suffocating her. She has a moment of realisation and clarity about her path. She knows she needs to live authentically. Her heart wants space and she sees she can only truly take care of herself. She feels great joy and peace and purpose at the end of the session.

5. Her relationships with her family are much better. They are stepping into their own power and taking care of themselves. She doesn't feel like she needs to be the head of the family any more. But she still feels blocked in her career.

We journey backwards through her life **using the breath** to get in touch with younger Christina who didn't want to survive. Lots of painful memories arise. Then we come back to her body now. Despite everything that has happened she is still here. She is alive. She has survived. We do a **meditation exercise** to imagine how she could live from this day forward, a beautiful future with joy, health and fulfillment. Then I ask her to imagine a river, flowing in the current direction. Ask for guidance to visualise what action she needs to take to cut a hole in the riverbank to allow water to start trickling on a different path, leading to that beautiful future. She gets really excited and happy because she sees very clearly what she needs to do. She feels she absolutely knows the next step.

Dina: three sessions over ten months

1. Dina works in a highly demanding job in the City of London and constantly pushes herself towards perfection in everything she does. She feels very stressed and exhausted.

I start with **Reiki** and then move to **hold her right arm and shoulder.** The limb wants to come across her body towards the left hand side. When it is **allowed a voice** it says that it wants to be more creative. Head responds that she is looking for a new job. Arm is not convinced that is enough – it wants to do something completely different!

Holding her head it wants to twist to quite an extreme position towards the right hand side and she can feel movement and adjustment the whole way down the right hand side of her neck and shoulder, where she suffers from chronic pain.

2. She has started a new job and has taken up some old hobbies again. But she is still suffering headaches and neck and shoulder pain.

I start with **craniosacral** work holding her head which

again wants to turn to the right. **I ask who is standing on the left** that she doesn't want to look at? She knows immediately it is a family member. As we focus on that person the pain in her neck intensifies and she realises she cannot solve that person's problems for them. We **place a rock on the neck** to represent what she is carrying for the other and then **imagine handing that back to them**. It does not belong to her. Then we continue with **body work** to release the stress in the neck and shoulders.

3. She is enjoying her hobbies and is doing far more things that give her pleasure so overall she is feeling really well, much less concerned and stressed, but she still suffers from headaches.

We do some further **releasing body work** and as I hold the left eye and a pressure point on the left shoulder the headache disappears. I do a **crystal extraction of dark energy** from her head via her ears. She realises she still needs to take better care of herself, get more rest and improve her diet.

Esther: three sessions over four months

1. Esther has a stressful job in the City of London. She has a bad relationship with her boss and sometimes just can't face going in to the office. She would like to quit but is scared. She admits she likes to be in control of things and is afraid of failure.

I start with **craniosacral** and feel a huge knot in the solar plexus area. I start **talking to different body parts**. The heart wants to leave the job but the head says that would be failure. Solar plexus wants to leave the job right now, today. I finish that session holding the feet and leading her in a masculine/feminine **balancing meditation.**

2. She reports that going to work is even worse now because she has become aware of how her body is feeling and the pain in the solar plexus and the heart. She is suffering heartburn. I **hold the solar plexus** and ask what is the repeating pattern she wants to avoid? She says she doesn't want to be rescued any more. There has been a pattern of

failing and then being rescued. At that point a lot of anger emerges. We **call in both the parents**, one at a time and dialogue with them.

She comes up with a **new contract** for life which feels good but is in complete contrast to what she is doing right now. I finish the session by giving her the **archetypes** in the chakras and explaining the **perceptual states**.

3. She doesn't care in the slightest about the job any more and hence is much more relaxed about her performance, although she is still there. She is able to delegate more and feels much less stressed. But she is aware she is not properly honouring the new contract for life that she took from the last session, or what she is capable of.

We start with looking at the possibility of resigning without knowing what she might then step into from the different **perceptual states**. In the place of serpent there is fear, but from the place of hummingbird she is really surprised, she imagines talking to those she is leaving behind about why she is going, trying to make a difference in how they might behave in the future and ensuring her departure is productive.

She then goes on the table and I hold the root, the place of fear. What is the worst that could happen? She realises that even the worst that could happen (to be unemployed for a little while) doesn't feel as bad as the pain she is in right now!

She sees that from all the different perspectives the best that could happen looks and feels amazing. The worst is really not so bad as it would be getting another similar job, which she is definitely able to do. But she doesn't really believe that's what would happen if she took the plunge to step into something that was much more in alignment with her new life contract. She feels much more relaxed, lighter, clearer. She knows what she has to do!

Francine: Three sessions over five months

1. Francine is an immigrant to the UK in her thirties who works as a cleaner although she has a university degree from back at home. She has chronic pain in the lower thoracic back

and feels very stressed about her sister being sick back at home whilst she is working here to try to make some money to send back to the family.

I **hold into the solar plexus** and ask what she can see. She replies 'All her black thoughts'. I ask her to **breathe** fully down into the belly and she starts to cry. I move to the head in a **craniosacral** hold and almost immediately the head wants to turn to the right. I ask **who or what is at the left shoulder that she doesn't want to look at**? She knows it is her father but there is nothing to say to him. He cannot forgive her.

I move to the heart. She can understand her father's pain and what keeps him stuck. He was very hurt. Actually she feels he has forgiven her but he just cannot say those words. The real problem is she cannot forgive herself. I ask her to feel into the heart. **What does it want to say, or want to be seen?** She doesn't want to voice it but she knows and is weeping.

We finish with one of her hands on the root and one on the heart. She is able to breathe between them a little and the solar plexus feels much lighter and she feels much more relaxed. She is amazed at what has emerged from listening to her body.

2. I start with **Reiki** and then I move to the solar plexus. What would it be like to give up trying to control everything and accept that she can only control her own reactions? She feels angry at that and then stressed – she logically knows that trying to control everything is not helpful, she can feel what happens when she floods her own system with stress hormones. I continue working through the body with Reiki and at the end she says she feels amazingly relaxed. She can see that the person she is harming most is herself.

3. She says she is far more observant now about how she reacts to things and she laughs about it when she notices she is trying to control things that she can't. Her family have become much closer as a result of her sister's illness and her father has become much more loving and communicative.

I start tuning in at the feet and then move again to the

solar plexus. I ask her to breathe to release all that is not normally allowed. Anger arises and I get a **pillow** and ask her to pound it for release. She still can't forgive herself.

When she lies down again I **hold the solar plexus** and ask who told her she has to be perfect? Her father. Who does she know that is perfect? Nobody! Does she love them despite that? Yes, in fact she loves their imperfections. So is it possible that she is lovable even although she is imperfect? Yes, that is OK!

She is able to **breathe** between the root and the heart chakra and the head feels good about feeling them and connecting with the body. She is able to **look at herself in the mirror** and sa 'I am not perfect and that is OK.'

Conclusion

'Early one morning before sunrise, a fisherman arrived at a river. On the bank he stumbled against something and found it to be a small sack of stones. He picked up the sack and putting his net aside, sat down on the bank to await the sunrise... Lazily he picked a stone out of the bag and threw it into the quiet river. Then he chose another stone and then another. In the silence of the early morning he liked the splashing sound, so he kept tossing the stones into the water one by one.

'Slowly the sun rose, it became light. By that time he had thrown all the stones away except one; the last stone lay in his palm. His heart almost failed him, he was breathless when he saw by the daylight what he held in his hand. It was a diamond! He had thrown a whole sack of them away; this was the last piece in his hand. He shouted, he cried. He had accidentally stumbled upon so much wealth that his life would have been enriched many times over. But in the darkness, unknowingly, he had thrown it all away.

'In a way that fisherman was fortunate, still one diamond was left; the light had dawned before he had thrown the last diamond too. Generally people are not even that fortunate. Their whole life passes and the sun never rises, the morning never comes in their lives. The light never comes, and they have thrown away all of life's diamonds thinking they were pebbles…

'It is very difficult for those who have already taken them (the treasures of life) to be pebbles to open their eyes and see that they are diamonds. And those who have wasted their lives in throwing them away as pebbles will be annoyed if you tell them that these are gems and not pebbles. They will flare up, not because what has been said is incorrect, but because they have been shown their own folly, because they have been reminded of how they have thrown away immense treasures.

'But no matter how much treasure has been lost, even if a single moment of life is still left, something can yet be salvaged. Something can still be known, something can still be attained. In the search of life,

it is never so late that one has to feel despair.'[112](Osho)

This is a long quote to open my Conclusion, but I just love this story! There is so much wisdom in it. We waste so much when we are in the darkness, asleep and unaware and we throw away so many gifts. There is so much beauty and potential in our hands if we choose to look and see it and recognise it. And there is always hope. Healing and resolution are always possible whilst there is breath in the body.

In the entangled inforealm every action, every word, every thought is energy moving, waves rippling, and has a consequence. The implication is that we need to take responsibility for the eternal ripples we create. We need to take responsibility for healing ourselves and our lineages, both karmic and genealogical.

What many teachers write of, based on millions of experiences across a range of societies and times, is that to live fulfilled, happy, healthy lives, we need to live honestly, with congruence between who we say we are and how we live. Villoldo teaches that part of authenticity is that the more you speak the truth the more of what you speak comes true. And part of responsibility is the need for integrity, as the more power we accumulate the deeper a hurtful word or action will go, the stronger its resonance in the holonomic brain will be.

It is also key for our own health to try to hold on to the beginner's mind, seeing things as if for the first time, making ourselves available for new experiences every day, knowing that we don't know. We don't want to get entangled and stuck in the stories, in the old attractor pathways, in the old beliefs that have now been superseded. We need to keep our minds open to new possibilities, new ways of thinking, new ways of being in the world. Things always change, that is one of the few certainties on our journey through life.

The new ways of thinking and working in Era III that I have described throughout this book present proof that

---

[112] Osho. 1973. *From Sex to Superconsciouness* St Martin's Press/Griffin, New York

healing can be quicker and wider than conventionally taught. I have also tried to explain to the best of my knowledge at this time, how and why these practices work. When we connect with the inforealm, limiting beliefs can be released instantaneously. Everything is possible, all knowledge is available and it is our intention and attention that collapse the probability wave into an observable event. That event may well come from the tail end of the distribution curve (it has a low probability, but is still a possibility). Shamans and other healers who can connect with the inforealm don't collude with the old stories, the old beliefs. Instead they help people to change their perspective to manifest immediate change at the mythical and energetic levels which is brought into the physical through ritual. They can ask for guidance and knowledge and receive the answer to any question.

At the same time when we connect with the omniscient and omnipotent entangled universe it is possible for us to reach out to the karmic and genealogical lineages, to bring peace and resolution to our past lives and the dead. This release for many generations of our ancestors can bring new levels of joy, peace and health to our current lives and helps prevent the entanglements and unresolved traumas being carried forward to the future generations. The work becomes truly transpersonal.

I want to finish this book by repeating a quotation from Laszlo that I used in Chapter 2. *'The recognition that the Akashic experience is a real and fundamental part of human experience has unparalleled importance for our time. When more people grasp the fact that they can have, and are perhaps already having, Akashic experiences, they will open their mind to them, and the experiences will occur more and more frequently, and to more and more people. A more evolved consciousness will spread in the world.'*[113]

My wish is that this book will encourage all who read it to dive into their own Akashic experiences in whatever way they find most accessible and then to talk about them and spread

---

[113] Laszlo, Ervin. 2009. *The Akashic Experience: Science and the Cosmic Memory Field* p.7 Rochester, Vermont, USA: Inner Traditions

this knowledge. It is time for all of us who have these experiences to share them, without fear or embarrassment. As we do so the willingness of others to experiment and question the system that keeps us small will increase and the pace of change within the medical and educational paradigms will accelerate.

I hope it will motivate you to risk stepping into the shadows to do your own healing work, shedding your limiting beliefs and societally induced judgements and connecting with your true potential. Then, if it draws you, expand your work to the ancestors. Finally, if you feel that is your path, take your place in the medicine circle of integrated healers, saying thank you for the joy and beauty of this life, in this body, at this time, on this amazing planet, when we are allowed to do this work on behalf of ourselves and those we encounter. Yes, I have choice. Yes, I am autonomous. Yes, I can be a part of the change that is very desperately needed on earth today.

Glossary

Affective neuroscience: the study of the neural mechanisms of emotion. Allied to affective psychotherapy, dealing with the emotional impact or affect of trauma.

Attractor: In mathematical theory, an attractor is a state towards which the system tends to evolve regardless of the starting conditions of the system. In neurology, the pathways of recognition are called limbic attractors.

Autonomy: The right or condition of self-government, freedom from external control or influence.

Ayahuasca: The Banisteriopsis caapi vine used in South America to prepare a hallucinogenic brew frequently called ayahuasca, but whose active ingredient is di-methyltryptamine, usually from Psychotria viridis leaves, known as chacruna. The ayahuasca plant itself provides the monoamine oxidase inhibitor, without which the DMT cannot be adequately absorbed by the brain.

Bardo: A resting or waiting place between human lifetimes.

Chakra: The energy centres inside and outside the body recognised in yoga and energy medicine. There are at least nine chakras - seven chakras starting within the body and reaching outwards in a cone shape through the various energy layers that surround the physical body, plus one below the feet and one above the crown.

Constellations psychotherapy: A systemic way of working, involving not only the client in isolation, but their whole system.

Craniosacral therapy: A therapy working with the individual's life force to establish a strong underlying vitality and the free flow of this inherent vitality throughout the body, thereby enabling the healing forces within to overcome disease and disturbance, and to release tensions and restrictions, so that symptoms, conditions and their underlying causes can be resolved.

Epigenetics: The science of how environmental signals select, modify and regulate gene activity leading to heritable changes in gene function that occur without a change in the DNA sequence.

Explicate order: The normal, large scale, three dimensional world.

Higher Self: The permanent self which survives after physical death, also known as the Atman. It can travel through space and time and can take up residence time after time in different human bodies to experience the realm of matter and thereby further its development or evolution.

Holonomic brain theory: A neurological model in which the distributed memory that exists throughout the brain is likened to a holographic storage network. This means that every piece of a long-term memory is distributed over the entire dendritic arbour in a neural hologram wherein each part of the network contains information about the whole event.

Implicate order: A term coined by Professor David Bohm to describe a model of the universe where each region contains a total structure enfolded within it.

Inforealm: The universal, omnipresent energy field which was traditionally called God, Brahman, Jehovah or Spirit, but which has been re-labelled in many different ways by specialists from different fields of science, medicine, biology and philosophy. For instance physicists may call it the holographic or entangled universe, the cosmic information field or the quantum vacuum. Parapsychologists label it the psi field. Constellations psychotherapists name it the knowing field.

Limbic resonance: Also known as empathic resonance, this is the theory that the capacity for sharing deep emotional states arises from the limbic system of the brain and that our brain chemistry and nervous systems are measurably affected by those closest to us – we resonate with them.

Mesa: The healing kit used by the Qero shamans of the Andes.

Neuroscience: The science of understanding the brain and the nervous system.

Non-locality: Instantaneous, coherent correlation between quanta separated by a distance large enough such that no signal could travel between them at light speed in the time allowed for the interaction.

Psychic dagger: Something harmful stuck in the energy field that was sent by another person, with or without conscious intention. Also known as a virote or poisoned dart.

Psychoneuroimmunology: The medical research which connects our thoughts (psyche), our nervous system (neurology) and our immune system.

Reiki: Literally translated, universal life force. A non-local method of healing at the physical, mental and emotional level, activated by intention and presence.

Remote viewing: The official term for the American 'Psychic Spying' programme that started at the Stanford Research Institute, (SRI) California, in 1973. It was conceived within and funded by the US Department of Defence and over time was known in the intelligence community as Grillflame, Centerlane, Starburst and Stargate. It taught people to view military targets psychically, at a different time and place from where they were physically located.

Shaman: A healer working with causes rather than symptoms, often in the energy field. Someone capable of altering their state of consciousness to work outside linear space and time.

Tantric yoga: A spiritual path for attaining enlightenment or union with the divine.

Temenos: a protected physical and emotional space in which the transforming work of healing takes place through learning and teaching.

Transgenerational body: the ongoing energetic impact in a family of what has happened to the ancestors, but could not be digested or healed at the time it occurred.

Yoni: the feminine sexual organs.

Bibliography

Bach, Richard. 2004. *Messiah's Handbook* Charlottesville, USA: Hampton Roads Publishing Company, Inc.

Bohm, David. 1980. *Wholeness and the Implicate Order* UK: Routledge & Paul Kegan

Broughton, Vivian. 2010. *In the Presence of Many* Frome, Somerset, UK: Green Balloon Publishing

Buxton, Simon. 2004. *The Shamanic Way of the Bee: Ancient Wisdom and Healing Practices of the Bee Masters* Rochester, Vermont, USA: Destiny Books a division of Inner Traditions International

Dossey, Larry, M.D. 1989. *Recovering the Soul: A Scientific and Spiritual Search* Bantam Doubleday Dell Publishing Group

Ferrucci, Piero. 1982. *What We May Be* New York, NY, USA: Jeremy P. Tarcher/Penguin

Franke, Ursula. 2003. *The River Never Looks Back. Historical and Practical Foundations of Bert Hellinger's Family Constellations* Heidelberg, Germany: Carl-Auer-Systeme Verlag

Hammer, Emanuel F. 1990. *Reaching the Affect: Style in the Psychodynamic Therapies* New York, USA: Jason Aronson, Inc.

Hausner, Stephan. 2011. *Even if it Costs me my Life: Systemic Constellations and Serious Illness* Santa Cruz, CA, USA: Gestalt Press, Taylor& Francis

Hellinger, Bert with ten Hovel, Gabriele. 1999. *Acknowledging What Is* Phoenix, Arizona, USA: Zeig, Tucker & Co., Inc.

Laszlo, Ervin. 2007. *Science and the Akashic Field: An Integral Theory of Everything* Rochester, Vermont, USA: Inner Traditions

Laszlo, Ervin. 2009. *The Akashic Experience: Science and the*

Cosmic Memory Field Rochester, Vermont, USA: Inner Traditions

Levine, Peter A. PhD. 2010. *In An Unspoken Voice: How the Body Releases Trauma and Restores Goodness* Berkeley, California, USA: North Atlantic Books

Lewis, Thomas, M.D., Aminin, Fari, M.D., Lannon, Richard, M.D. 2000. *A General Theory of Love* New York, USA: Vintage Books, Random House

Mason Boring, Francesca. 2012 *Connecting to Our Ancestral Past: Healing through Family Constellations, Ceremony, and Ritual* Berkeley, California USA: North Atlantic Books

McGilchrist, Iain. 2009. *The Master and his Emissary: The Divided Brain and the Making of the Western World* New Haven and London: Yale University Press

Osho. 1973. *From Sex to Superconsciousness* St Martin's Press/Griffin, New York, copyright Osho International Foundation, Switzerland, www.OSHO.com

Osho, 2000. *New Man for the New Millennium* Osho International Foundation, www.OSHO.com/copyrights

Osho. 1974. *The Book of Secrets: 112 Meditations to Discover the Mystery Within* New York, NY, USA: Osho International Foundation

Pert, Ph.D., Candace B. 1999. *Molecules of Emotion, Why You Feel the Way You Feel* London, U.K.: Simon & Schuster

Pert, PhD., Candace B. 2006. *Everything You Need To Know To Feel Good* London, UK: Hay House

Roth, Gabrielle. 1989. *Maps to Ecstasy* Mill Valley, CA, USA: Nataraj Publishing

Ruppert, Franz. 2012. *Symbiosis & Autonomy, Symbiotic Trauma and Love Beyond Entanglements* Steyning, UK: Green Balloon Publishing

Schneider, Jakob Robert. 2007. *Family Constellations: Basic Principles and Procedures* Heidelberg, Germany: Carl-Auer-Systeme Verlag

Schore, Allan N. 2012. *The Science of the Art of Psychotherapy* New York, USA, W.W. Norton & Company

Shealy, M.D., Ph.D., Norman and Church Ph.D., Dawson. 2008. *Soul Medicine: Awakening your Inner Blueprint for Abundant Health and Energy* USA: Energy Psychology Press

Sheldrake, Rupert, McKenna, Terence and Abraham, Ralph. 1992. *Chaos, Creativity and Consciousness* Rochester, Vermont, USA: Park Street Press

Sheldrake, Rupert. 2013. *The Science Delusion* London, UK: Coronet, Hodder & Stoughton Ltd.

Siegel, Daniel J. 2010. *The Mindful Therapist, A Clinician's Guide to Mindsight and Neural Integration* New York, USA: W.W. Norton & Company, Inc.

Singh Khalsa, M.D., Dharma and Stauth, Cameron. 2001. *Meditation as Medicine* New York, NY, USA: Fireside

Stein, Diane. 1995. *Essential Reiki: A complete guide to an ancient healing art* Freedom, CA, USA: The Crossing Press, Inc.

Tolle, Eckhart. 1999. *The Power of Now* USA: New World Library

Van Lommel, Pim. 2011. *Consciousness Beyond Life: The Science of the Near-Death Experience* Harper One

Villoldo, Ph.D., Alberto. 2005. *Mending the Past and Healing the Future with Soul Retrieval* Carlsbad, CA, USA: Hay House, Inc.

Useful websites

Conscious Dying
http://www.dyingconsciously.org

Dr Larry Dossey
http://www.dosseydossey.com

Masuru Emoto
http://www.masaru-emoto.net/english/water-crystal.html

Stuart Hameroff
http://www.quantumconsciousness.org/personal.html

Monroe Institute
http://www.monroeinstitute.org/

Ananda Sarita
http://www.ananda-sarita.com

Soul Medicine Institute
http://www.soulmedicineinstitute.org/home.html

Alberto Villoldo
http://thefourwinds.com

Roger Woolger
http://www.deepmemoryprocess.com